AN INTIMATE LOOK AT SKATING'S GREATEST TOUR

AN INTIMATE LOOK AT SKATING'S GREATEST TOUR

TEXT BY BARRY WILNER

Introduction by Scott Hamilton

A LIONHEART BOOK

Andrews McMeel
Publishing

Kansas City

STARS ON ICE

For information, write Andrews McMeel Publishing, an Andrews McMeel Universal Company, 4520 Main Street, Kansas City, Missouri 64111.

www.andrewsmcmeel.com

98 99 00 01 02 TRC 10 9 8 7 6 5 4 3 2 1
Library of Congress Cataloging-in-Publication Data on file

Stars on Ice is a production of

Executive Producers: Robert D. Kain and Gary V. Swain
Producers: Scott Hamilton and Byron Allen
Co-Producer/Director: Sandra Bezic
Co-Director: Michael Seibert
Associate Director: Lea Ann Miller
Choreographers: Sandra Bezic, Michael Seibert, Jayne Torvill & Christopher Dean, and Lea Ann Miller

Produced by Lionheart Books, Ltd.
Atlanta, Georgia 30341

Project Director: Michael Reagan
Design: Carley Wilson Brown
Editorial Director: Deborah Murphy
Cover photo: Heinz Kluetmeier

To Sergei Grinkov and Rob McCall

ACKNOWLEDGMENTS

A project of this magnitude could not go smoothly without the assistance of many people. We would like to acknowledge the contributions of everyone involved with Stars on Ice, from the skaters to the support staff, especially Sandra Bezic and Scott Hamilton, and of course Heinz Kluetmeier whose photography is an important part of this book.

Our heartfelt thanks go to the staff at IMG, particularly Bob Kain, Gary Swain, Byron Allen, Deb Nast, David Chalfant, David Baden, Michael Merrall, Jay Ogden, and especially Tami Hahn for her encyclopedic knowledge of the photography archives.

Special thanks to Susan Lohman who brilliantly choreographed the complex flow of information that made this book possible.

We would also like to recognize the assistance of Marie Millikan, Nancy Armour, Heather Linhart, Michael Sterling, Kevin Albrecht, Martha Henderson, Yuki Saegusa, Jessica Nardo, and the unwavering guidance of Lynn Plage.

TABLE OF CONTENTS

INTRODUCTION

We have given the best in the world a place to take their skating far beyond what they were able do as competitive athletes. A place where we aren't presenting just skating but the best of what we are and hope to be. For you.

Scott Hamilton

Stars on Ice started out in a unique way. Like most successful undertakings, it came out of an experiment. It also came out of desperation. I had just gotten "released" from Ice Capades and was in need of a place to work. Two years out of the Olympics, I still had a few axels and salchows left in me.

What you are about to see and read is an account of how when you are given "broken eggs" you make an omelette.

The Olympic figure skating "Class of 84" was a very special one: Torvill & Dean, Katarina Witt, Brian Orser, Brian Boitano, Rosalynn Sumners, Peter & Kitty Carruthers, Jozef Sabovcek, Underhill and Martini, myself and many others skated for the challenge and opportunities that came with hard work.

We loved what we did and saw things in the sport that, possibly, others didn't. The traditional shows were starting to run out of fresh ideas and were getting to a point of being "corporate." Each year was just that, another year, and many of the skaters were looking to break ground and try something new.

I once heard, and now live by, the philosophy that "The only thing that grows in an inactive career is an ego." The traditional shows were competing, not so much to create new directions, but for buildings and schedules to remain financially successful.

Thus, an opportunity presented itself—an opportunity to create something that a sophisticated, newly educated and growing audience was ready to support. An opportunity that a hungry, ambitious, rebellious and special group of champions was ready to undertake that would break ground and take touring skating in a whole new direction.

Many shows came out of that "Class of 84". Torvill & Dean went straight from their amateur skating and created something very much in their image. The Tour of Olympic and World Figure Skating Champions had record audiences after the "1984 season," and an exciting attitude was growing that would find its way into meeting rooms of people that could make things happen. All of these factors played a very significant role in the creation and growth of Stars on Ice.

The song "We Didn't Start the Fire" by Billy Joel shows that the present grows out of the past; history has a tendency to repeat itself. Stars on Ice isn't necessarily the first show with an attitude of this kind. Think back to Sonja Henie and the shows that she created and how she took the world by storm. All any sport needs are engaging personalities to bring people in, and that is how Stars on Ice started and has continued to grow since its inception.

We have given the best in the world a place to take their skating far beyond what they were able do as competitive athletes. A place where we aren't presenting just skating but the best of what we are and hope to be. For you.

This book chronicles our history and gives you a peek backstage into a tour that has changed skating for the present and has "raised the bar" for future shows. We love what we do and only want to share the best of all of that with you. Because without you, none of this could exist.

Thank you for all the years and for an incredible future.

"What you are about to see and read is an account of how when you are given 'broken eggs' you make an omelette."

1997-'98 STARS ON ICE

CAST & CREW

(front row seated—left to right) EKATERINA GORDEEVA, BRIAN ORSER, KIM SCOTT–*wardrobe*, ALAN HERRO–*assistant production manager*, DAVID FINLEY–*lighting director*, MIMI ENGLISH–*lighting crew*, JESSICA NARDO–*operations assistant*, KEN BILLINGTON–*lighting designer*; *(second row—left to right)* DAVID HOFFIS–*production manager*, KATARINA WITT, ROSALYNN SUMNERS, JEF BILLINGS–*costume design*, PAUL WYLIE, RENÉE ROCA, SCOTT HAMILTON, KRISTI YAMAGUCHI, ELENA BECHKE, GEORGE REEVES–*lighting crew*, LEA ANN MILLER–*associate director*, JASON KANTROWITZ–*associate lighting director*, MARVIN DOLGAY–*music director*, SANDRA BEZIC–*co-producer/director*; *(third row—left to right)* DENIS PETROV, MARTINA SCHMELOVA–*treatment therapist*, GORSHA SUR, BRAD MALKUS–*lighting programmer*, KURT BROWNING, LIBBY GRAY–*lighting crew*, DEB NAST–*talent/media coordinator*, SCOTT HARVEY–*sound engineer*, BYRON ALLEN–*producer*, MICHAEL SEIBERT–*co-director*, DAVID BADEN–*tour director*

CHAPTER ONE

GETTING STARTED

"I had imagined after all the work you put into training for competitions . . . well, maybe there was a paradise for skaters at the end of that."

Scott Hamilton

Scott Hamilton sat on the beach and worried. His career was over, he thought. There was no place for him on the ice anymore. There was room for the Smurfs and Disney characters. Plenty of space for the women stars, the Dorothy Hamills and Peggy Flemings.

But a male figure skater, even the most recent gold medalist, a true American hero who had overcome childhood disease and personal setbacks, was locked out.

"I was pretty bummed out about it," Scott said. "I had imagined after all the work you put into training for competitions as an amateur working toward the Olympics, well, maybe I thought there was a paradise for skaters at the end of that."

Actually, Scott's professional career had begun pretty well. After winning his fourth straight world championship—following four consecutive U.S. titles and, of course, the 1984 Olympic gold medal—Scott met with Bob Kain of IMG. Scott, naturally, was seeking something substantial (creatively and financially) after dominating the amateur skating world.

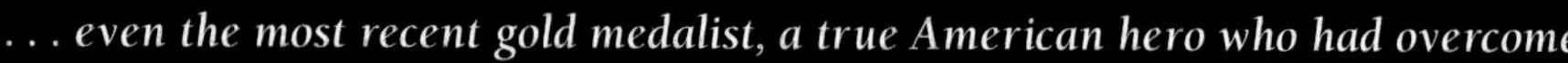

. . . even the most recent gold medalist, a true American hero who had overcome childhood disease and personal setbacks, was locked out.

BARBARA UNDERHILL & PAUL MARTINI

"The first thing I did as his manager was go see him on the Tom Collins tour while he still had amateur status," Kain recalled. IMG was the major player among tennis representatives then, and Kain was working with Bjorn Borg and Vitas Gerulaitis. The night before the Collins tour show, Kain and Borg and Gerulaitis spent most of the night partying with Scott.

"He had to skate the next day and I could barely walk," Kain said. "But he came out in Joe Louis Arena with a Red Wings jersey on, and 15,000 people were standing and screaming. That was the first skating event I went to, and when he skated, everyone went crazy. I said to myself, 'This is pretty cool.' I asked him why he just didn't go skate in Tom Collins' tour every year? Then I found out about the rules." Once Scott turned pro, he could not be on the same ice with the amateurs.

Ever since he became a world-class skater, Scott imagined performing in a troupe of just skaters. No Smurfs. No Mickey Mouse. No Cowardly Lions.

At a news conference in that hotbed of figure skating, Atlantic City, New Jersey, Scott announced his move into the professional ranks. He joined Ice Capades.

"It was a logical thing to do," he said. "There wasn't a lot of choice—things weren't anything like they are now."

For two years, things went reasonably well for Scott, but sharing the ice with cartoon characters was hardly his idea of taking skating to another level. He was making a living as a skater and enjoying himself, but it wasn't particularly challenging.

The biggest challenge, of course, was just ahead.

In 1986, Kain met with the new owner of Ice Capades, Tom Scallen. In no uncertain terms, Scallen told him Scott was out.

"Men don't sell tickets in figure skating," was Scallen's point-blank explanation.

Kain flew to Florida and sat on the Delray Beach sand, explaining to Scott what went down with Ice Capades.

"What am I going to do?" Scott said. "Dorothy [Hamill] has done Ice Capades for ten years. And now I don't have a job?"

Well, true. But he had a vision.

Ever since becoming a world-class skater, Scott had imagined performing in a troupe of just skaters. No Smurfs. No Mickey Mouse. No Scarecrows and Cowardly Lions.

He foresaw ensembles, interaction among the skaters, themed production numbers, interplay with the audience. So he set about creating just such a show.

"But this was going to be a real challenge," Scott maintained, "because the skaters would carry so much of the show."

Kain certainly was willing to give it a try: "I said, 'Why not do for the pros what Tom Collins does with the amateurs? You and Rosalynn [Sumners] and Kitty and Peter Carruthers and Michael [Seibert] and Judy [Blumberg] are the ones they are screaming for. You're the '84 Olympic class.'"

KATHLEEN SCHMELZ

Kain said IMG would be willing to underwrite the venture, and the creative process would rest in the hands of Scott, the other skaters he would choose for the tour, and whomever he wanted to hire to direct the shows.

Kain would become the executive producer. He hired Gary Swain, whose main client was John McEnroe, to become Director of the tour. Swain had extensive experience with such tours—in tennis and basketball. He had produced, promoted, and staged a 99 city tour for McEnroe and IMG tennis clients and an NBA All-Stars Tour that featured Michael Jordan's first professional basketball game.

"I didn't know anything about skating," Swain said, "but I knew about creating events. I realized that this tour would feature skaters in a way they'd never been seen before. It would showcase the athletic and artistic aspects of skating, and the skaters' personalities. I saw that there was room for a very high quality production with sound, lights, choreography, and top-notch world-class skating—touring on an annual basis." It was such a good idea that Swain was surprised it had never been done. "What convinced me it would work is the skaters already have an international marketing platform, the Olympics. And the amount of TV exposure the Olympics offered for these skaters, who in winning their medals and stepping on the podium

"Skaters are very creative people. We all have ideas in our minds on things we'd like to attempt, ways to take our skating to a new artistic level and keep finding challenges. This was going to be a real challenge, because the skaters would carry so much of the show."

became instant celebrities and well-known athletes, was phenomenal.

"Plus, people are attracted to figure skating who are not necessarily your traditional sports fans. The music and costumes attract them; it's like theater and a concert."

The folks at IMG were not about to get ahead of themselves, however. They would not book Madison Square Garden and the LA Forum right away. They would not schedule 60-city tours from Portland, Maine, to Portland, Oregon. They would start small, gauge the public's reaction, then move on.

To join Scott as a headliner, they hired Rosalynn Sumners, who won a silver medal behind Katarina Witt at Sarajevo. Rosalynn had had a miserable two years touring with Disney's skating show. She was prepared to quit altogether.

"I'm not cut out for 14 shows a week, twice each day, and that grind was getting to me," Roz said. "I wasn't training the way I needed to and I wasn't skating the way I wanted to.

"I took a few months off, just got away from the ice, and I wasn't sure I'd ever go back. Then Scott called—I was one of the first people he contacted. He knew exactly what was missing for me. He knew I'd get a boost from the tour."

ROSALYNN SUMNERS

"I took a few months off, just got away from the ice, and I wasn't sure I'd ever go back. Then Scott called. . . .He knew exactly what was missing for me. He knew I'd get a boost from the tour."

Still, Roz wasn't sure; she was still feeling burned out. But ultimately Scott persuaded her to sign on for the proposed five-city tour.

Also hired were Judy Blumberg and Michael Seibert, the U.S. dance champions while Scott was winning his American singles crowns; Canadian stars Toller Cranston and Brian Pockar; Sandy Lenz; and Lisa Carey and her partner, Chris Harrison.

Entitled the "Scott Hamilton America Tour," the show would debut in Orono, Maine. From there, it would travel to Burlington, Vermont; Durham, New Hampshire; Morristown, New Jersey; and Philadelphia. All of the venues were small, mostly on college campuses. The travel schedule was pretty brutal—five cities in five nights. Production costs were minimal.

Near-disasters weren't.

"Now, I'm an expert," Kain said with a chuckle. "I say to Scott, I figure we can just use spotlights, trying to save on the budget. Scott says no way, we've got to do it right and got to have lights.

"We went out and hired a lighting guy from a rock 'n' roll tour and got all these lights strung up and down the side of the hockey arena at the University of Maine. The show begins, and it's great. The place loves it.

"We have these big wires running out to a generator, and during the finale some of those wires break and start spewing sparks into the crowd. But the people think we have fireworks to end the show, and they're really impressed."

Except for the ones being zapped by the sparks. Eleven people were sent to the hospital, according to Kain, "fortunately for minor burns. If we had been in New York, everyone would have sued us for millions and we never would have had another show. It was really a local electrician, but we felt stupid and looked stupid."

Swain had to be in Nashville to participate in a trial regarding John McEnroe during the "Scott Hamilton Tour" and missed all the fun.

They would start small, gauge the public's reaction, then move on.

"SCOTT HAMILTON AMERICA TOUR" *(left to right)*—TOLLER CRANSTON, CHRIS HARRISON, SANDY LENZ, SCOTT HAMILTON, ROSALYNN SUMNERS, MICHAEL SEIBERT, BRIAN POCKAR, JUDY BLUMBERG, & LISA CAREY.

ROSALYNN SUMNERS, SANDY LENZ, JUDY BLUMBERG, & LISA CAREY

"It might sound comical now, but it was pretty upsetting then," he said. "When I hung up the phone, I just said, 'Things need to be better in Burlington.'"

Of course, they wouldn't be.

No, the lights would not explode and sparks would not fly into the crowd. Instead, at midafternoon, it looked as if there would be no lights at all. And no show.

The crew hired by IMG had taken down the lights in Orono and driven them to the University of Vermont in Burlington, but the entire staff at the arena that was supposed to put up the lights and equipment had failed to show up.

"I go to Scott—this was my biggest fear—and I said we've got to go with spotlights only. He was upset. So I go to the bank, and with my MasterCard I get $2,500 worth of fifties. Then we go hand out money to get a bunch of kids from the school to put the lights up in two hours."

From such humble beginnings come . . . more humbling experiences.

The University of Vermont was known then for its strong hockey teams, and the figure skaters were not given access to the team's locker room. The visiting team's locker room was the only facility made available, and all of the skaters, male and female, had to dress in it.

Kain spent much of the hour preceding the opening number hanging a curtain between the men and women, and by intermission it had sagged to waist-high.

The visiting team's locker room was the only facility made available, and all of the skaters, male and female, had to dress in it. Kain spent much of the hour preceding the opening number hanging a curtain between the men and women. . . .

BOB KAIN & YUKI SAEGUSA

But the skaters weren't sagging.

"You learn to deal with adversities like that, and they bring you closer together," Scott said. "We didn't expect everything to go perfectly right off. And we all felt this was something we could build, so even with some really strange things happening, we never lost our spirit."

Things went far more smoothly in the next three shows. No unplanned pyrotechnics. No absent workers. No coed locker rooms.

Karen Kresge, the director of those early shows—and of Stars on Ice until 1992—remembers those mishaps and misadventures. But, for her, they are overshadowed by the professionalism of the performers and their willingness to try something different.

"I had had a lot of experience putting shows together and doing group choreography, which essentially is what I was there for, but this was definitely unknown territory. I was working with Olympic champions who had trained alone and skated alone. Here I came, trying to teach more complex choreography. Some people were used to it, others not.

"But they all had so much spirit and such a desire to make it work, that it seemed we could overcome whatever obstacles there were."

Karen Kresge, the director of those early shows—and of Stars on Ice until 1992—remembers those mishaps and misadventures. But, for her, they are overshadowed by the professionalism of the performers. . . ."They all had so much spirit and such a desire to make it work, that it seemed we could overcome whatever obstacles there were."

By the end of the five-city endeavor, IMG was optimistic. This was a winner. Packaging it correctly, publicizing it well, and working out the kinks were the next key steps.

"It was evident from Day One these skaters loved what they were doing, and whoever came to see a show left with their expectations totally exceeded," Swain said. "The fans were coming, I believe, to see the stars, but we gave them a totally different look and a show that received really excellent response from the audience. This was something that could really grow."

Kain believed another market test was necessary, and a second five-city tour was scheduled for December. This time, the sites were somewhat bigger—Wichita, Kansas; St. Paul, Minnesota; Lansing, Michigan; Hamilton, Ontario; and Buffalo, New York. The arenas were bigger, ranging in size from approximately 7,000 to 17,000 in the new Copps Coliseum in Hamilton.

So were some of the names, as the cast was bolstered with the likes of Olympic champions Hamill and Robin Cousins, plus the dynamic pair Jo Jo Starbuck and Ken Shelley.

"We were in our research mode," Kain said. "We went to bigger cities and were trying to get a different feel. We wanted to build a tour to last."

To establish such a tour, everyone agreed a permanent name was needed.

KAREN KRESGE

(back—left to right) ELAINE ZAYAK, BILL FAUVER, LEA ANN MILLER, TOLLER CRANSTON, ROSALYNN SUMNERS, SCOTT HAMILTON, BOB KAIN, JUDY BLUMBERG, MICHAEL SEIBERT, DOROTHY HAMILL, BRIAN POCKAR, KATHLEEN SCHMELZ, *(front—left to right)* GARY SWAIN, YUKI SAEGUSA, AND PRODUCTION PERSONNEL FROM LIVE LIGHT PRODUCTIONS.

"We were shooting for the biggest and best names in the skating world, all in one tour."

Kain, Swain, and several other managers didn't feel Scott's—or anyone's—name should be carried in the title.

"We didn't think Scott's name was the way to last," Kain said. "If there is one superstar and he hurts himself, you have to close. We were shooting for the biggest and best names in the skating world, all in one tour."

They tossed around several ideas, but ultimately, only two possibilities fit: Stars on Ice, or Champions on Ice.

"Stars was simple, and we thought it portrayed our show best," Swain said. "Obviously we would not be permitted to use the Olympic name in any way, shape, or form, so we had to create something outside of that. Yet we did feature Olympic and world champion skaters."

They featured Stars–and, they hoped, an expanding galaxy.

Stars on Ice it was.

SCOTT HAMILTON, "SCREWY MUSIC"

CHAPTER TWO

GETTING ESTABLISHED

"The most important thing was the idea that we would make *Stars on Ice* a show to last . . . It had to grow."

Bob Kain—executive producer

On the last day of January 1987, Stars on Ice hit the road. Medium-size cities in the East and Midwest were targeted, and the Stars on Ice banner flew at arenas in upstate New York (Rochester and Syracuse), in Fort Wayne, Indiana, in Battle Creek and Muskegon, Michigan, and in Toledo, Ohio.

Three previous mini-tours convinced IMG and the skaters that they were on the right track. But to stage a longer, more varied tour, a corporate sponsor was needed.

IMG wanted to take the show to at least 30 cities. It presented that concept in the corporate marketplace and found two eager sponsors in Discover Card and Chrysler.

Discover Card was only beginning to make inroads in the credit card field. It wasn't nearly as established as MasterCard or Visa and didn't have the advertising budget of its competitors. But it sought to enhance its name awareness nationally, and a skating tour headlined by Scott Hamilton, Dorothy Hamill, and Rosalynn Sumners was a very effective way to do so.

"Ultimately," said Benny Lawrence, marketing manager for Discover Card,

"It started as a tour by the skaters for the skaters, so we were doing much of our own stuff. That made it unique."—Bill Fauver

Discover Card was only beginning to make inroads in the credit card field. It wasn't nearly as established as MasterCard or Visa and didn't have the advertising budget of its competitors. But it sought to enhance its name awareness nationally, and a skating tour headlined by Scott Hamilton, Dorothy Hamill, and Rosalynn Sumners was a very effective way to do so.

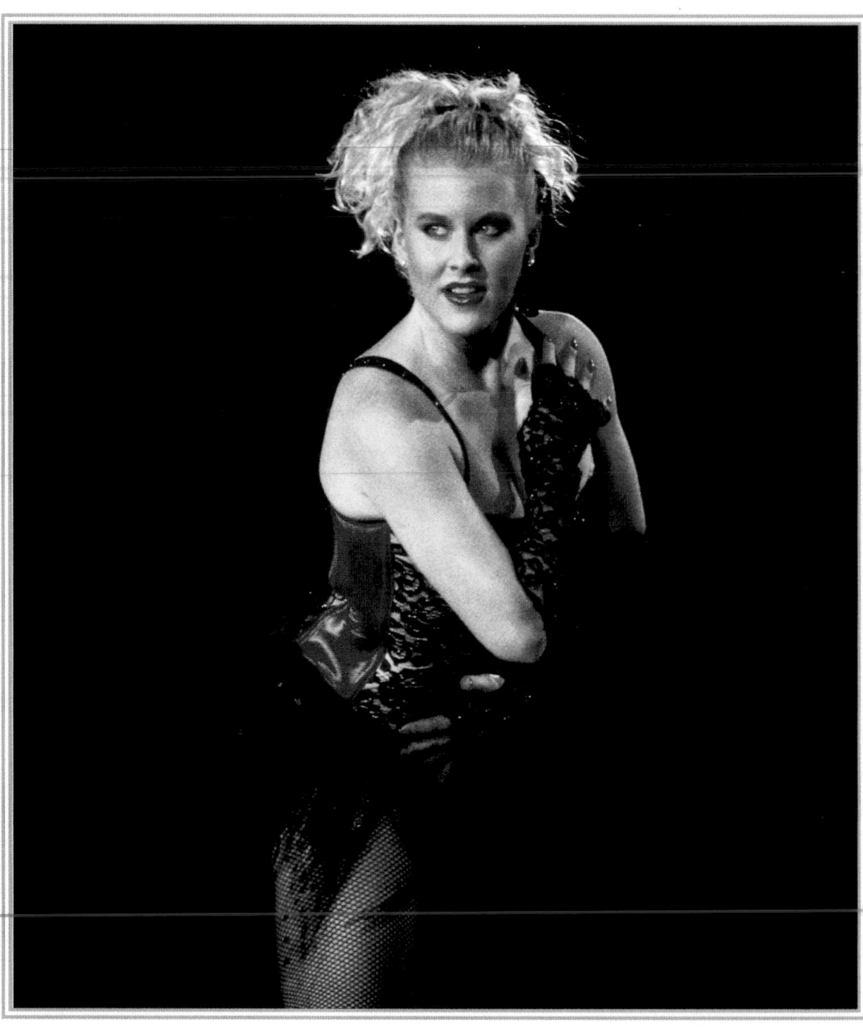

ROSALYNN SUMNERS, "MOTOWN REVUE"

"it turned out to be a great way not only to get the Discover Card name out, but to reinforce what Discover Card stands for."

Discover Card became the title sponsor for the 1987–88 tour, and Plymouth came aboard as the presenting sponsor—a relationship that didn't last in the United States, but continues in Canada with Chrysler.

But gaining sponsorship did not solve all the problems of Stars on Ice. Timing, for instance, was working against the success of the tour.

Stars on Ice would visit 34 cities, beginning in Denver on September 25, 1987, and concluding in Greensboro, North Carolina, on January 9, 1988. While most of the venues had increased in size, touring in those months was a negative.

The fourth quarter of any year always means competition—from the holidays, with media attention generally more difficult to obtain; from other forms of entertainment, particularly from the movie industry around Thanksgiving and through Christmas; from sports (especially football); even from politics during election years.

"We wanted to carve our niche from January through March," Swain said. But that would take a while. The first full-scale tour featured Americans Scott, Rosalynn, Dorothy, Judy Blumberg and Michael Seibert, Lea Ann Miller and partner Billy Fauver, and Kathleen Schmelz. Plus, from Canada, Toller Cranston, Brian Pockar, Barbara Underhill, and Paul Martini.

What it would be about on the ice was professionalism and superb entertainment. . . .

"We were taking our first really big steps now," Scott recalled. "We'd had our ups and downs and little adventures starting out, and now we wanted to establish what Stars on Ice would be all about."

What it would be about on the ice was professionalism and superb entertainment—a unique experience that, in the tradition of show business at any level, kept them coming back for more.

What it was about off the ice, at times, was chaos.

There was, for example, the time Dorothy decided she needed a hair cut. Because she was as well known for the Hamill cut as for the Hamill camel, Dorothy needed to see her private hairstylist, who was in Vail.

But the tour was heading to Milwaukee. Dorothy flew to Vail for the necessary trim, then took a plane back to Chicago—where she was told all flights to Milwaukee were canceled by a blizzard in Wisconsin.

IMG arranged for a limo to pick her up at O'Hare Airport and drive her to the arena in Milwaukee.

"We were all looking around, asking where Dorothy was," Rosalynn recalled. "The show was about to begin, we were all in costume and the lights were going to go down, and in she ran.

"I think that was the closest we came to not having somebody there for one of the early shows."

But it was hardly the only unusual occurrence.

Lynn Plage, the tour's publicist from Day One, has seen—and done—it all.

What it was about off the ice, at times, was chaos. . . . Because she was as well known for the Hamill cut as for the Hamill camel, Dorothy needed to see her private hairstylist, who was in Vail. But the tour was heading for Milwaukee. . . .

"I zipped up costumes, ran out and got props, bought bottled water. I used to tell everyone I was allergic to needle and thread, but I took care of some costumes, hung drapes.

"I remember pulling into a hotel in Ames, Iowa, and there was snow in the hallways and we had to trek our own luggage through. The sign outside the hotel said, 'Welcome to the 4H Clubs of America.' And here we were, all these Olympic skaters and champions and they did not even have us listed."

To boost ticket sales and make fans aware of their presence, the skaters would do media days. Lots of media days.

IMG would rent cars or find a skating club parent who was interested in driving skaters around a city. Plage would book as many interviews as possible in one day, sometimes not leaving time for breaks or lunches. Once, Scott asked a limo driver to go to the drive-through window at a Roy Rogers so he could order a quick meal.

Rosalynn did 15 media days one year, a tour record. On one of those—she wouldn't say where—she was interviewed by a TV anchor who thought she was a roller skater.

(clockwise from top) LYNN PLAGE & HEINZ KLUETMEIER, LYNN PLAGE & SCOTT HAMILTON, LYNN PLAGE & ROSALYNN SUMNERS

Rosalynn did 15 media days one year, a tour record. On one of those—she wouldn't say where—she was interviewed by a TV anchor who thought she was a roller skater.

In Chicago, Kitty and Peter Carruthers were scheduled for a media day and a huge snowstorm hit. People abandoned their cars in the streets as the city came to a standstill. Peter couldn't get into the city, so Kitty did all the interviews from her hotel room by phone.

For a media day in Richmond, where ticket sales were lagging, Scott and Plage boarded a plane at 6:00 a.m. The second they arrived, Scott was whisked off to a makeshift rink with a leaky roof that was open all around.

"When he did a back flip," Plage said, "we thought he would go through the roof."

It was not exactly what Lea Ann Miller, who remains with Stars on Ice as a choreographer, and Bill Fauver (who left the tour in '92) had in mind when they joined Stars in 1987.

"We had just finished the Torvill and Dean show, competed at the world professionals, and Scott knew us from Colorado," Lea Ann said. "We were just excited to have a job. There were not a lot of opportunities at that time out there. It was nice to see IMG supporting Scott and his idea."

EKATERINA GORDEEVA & SERGEI GRINKOV

IMG was supportive. . . but also figured Stars on Ice would get a major boost by, well, adding some more stars on the ice in 1988. With the Calgary Olympics lifting skating into the spotlight again—most notably the Battle of the Brians, the Dueling Carmens, and the ascension of Ekaterina Gordeeva and Sergei Grinkov to the pairs summit—the show could benefit by bringing in some new blood, headliners from the 1988 Games.

ROB McCALL & TRACY WILSON, "BILLION DOLLAR BABY"

"Back then, we had fewer members to work with and were on the ice seven to eight times a show," said Fauver, "and everybody was very involved in all that went on, whether it was a group number or somebody else's solo."

"It started as a tour by the skaters for the skaters, so we were doing much of our own stuff. That made it unique. . . . The atmosphere was very supportive, a family-type group.

"Back then, we had fewer members to work with and were on the ice seven to eight times a show, and everybody was very involved in all that went on, whether it was a group number or somebody else's solo."

IMG was supportive, too, but also figured Stars on Ice would get a major boost by adding some more stars on the ice in 1988. With the Calgary Olympics lifting skating into the spotlight again—most notably the Battle of the Brians, the Dueling Carmens, and the ascension of Ekaterina Gordeeva and Sergei Grinkov to the pairs summit—the show could benefit by bringing in some new blood, headliners from the '88 Games.

Figure skating was beginning to grow in popularity by 1988, although not nearly the way it would explode in the 1990s. The Calgary Olympics were such a spectacular showcase for Brian Boitano, Brian Orser, Katarina Witt, Debi Thomas, Canada's Liz Manley, and Russians Gordeeva and Grinkov that the public thirst for more was whetted.

"Those were the first Olympics after the Scott Hamilton America Tour," Kain said. "It was imperative that some of the stars of that Olympics come with us."

But Boitano and Witt, the gold medalists, began their own tour, under the auspices of Bill Graham Presents. Graham, who once ran the Fillmore East and West, was considered the premier entertainment entrepreneur of his day. For the first time—and as they headed into only their second full season—IMG and Stars on Ice had some very serious competition.

All of a sudden, according to Kain, there was one tour too many. "And Bill Graham Presents is pretty rough competition. Especially when they have the two hot ones out of the Olympics, that is formidable. Plus, he knows all the building operators and how to get the dates, so we are in a dogfight. We had to go head-to-head with them for two years."

Still, Stars on Ice clearly was progressing. The versatility in the performances increased with the addition of Kitty and Peter Carruthers in 1989 after Orser, Thomas, Tracy Wilson, and Rob McCall joined the previous year. There were some wonderful production numbers, including one created by Scott and musical collaborator Rick Neilsen of Cheap Trick called "Man of Many Colors." Scott lands on the Planet of Black and White and must defeat evil by giving everyone a dash of color. He pulls out a backpack of rainbow silk and illuminates the entire planet. According to Scott "There has never been another number like it, and we could not have pulled it off without Rick's music and Dennis St. John's great production skills.

Kresge, Scott, and the others also turned to more popular music, including

SCOTT HAMILTON AS "MAN OF MANY COLORS" WITH TOLLER CRANSTON AS THE "EVIL WIZARD"

Stars on Ice clearly was progressing. The versatility in the performances increased with the addition of Kitty and Peter [Carruthers] in 1989 after Orser, Thomas, Tracy Wilson, and Rob McCall joined the previous year. And there were some wonderful production numbers in the 1987–'88 season, including one created by Scott called "Man of Many Colors. . . ."

KITTY & PETER CARRUTHERS

MILLER AND FAUVER

"We had just finished the Torvill and Dean show, competed at the world professionals. . . .We were just excited to have a job. There were not a lot of opportunities at that time out there."

works by the Beatles and Andrew Lloyd-Webber in 1988, and a wonderful Salsa routine in '89.

Lea Ann got to try her hand at developing a group number, as well. She had some experience in choreography, and having grown up in St. Louis, she had a strong attachment to baseball.

"As a kid, I fell asleep in the back seat of the car listening to Jack Buck broadcast Cardinals games," she recalled. "So we had him record this piece for us that we called 'Casey at the Bat.' There was all this great baseball music, stuff from 'Damn Yankees,' and elsewhere. And we wanted to use Debi's great sense of humor in it, put her at the center of it all.

"Scott is a smart producer and he knew that to make it successful, he

BRIAN ORSER, "HIT THE ROAD JACK"

1992-93 ENSEMBLE PRODUCTION, "JUMP", *(left to right)* PAUL WYLIE, SCOTT HAMILTON, GARY BEACOM, KITTY CARRUTHERS, PETER CARRUTHERS, ROSALYNN SUMNERS, BRIAN ORSER, SERGEI GRINKOV, & EKATERINA GORDEEVA

The baseball number was a showstopper in 1991–92. It also provided the impetus for the wonderful, full-cast ensemble productions that would follow.

needed to be in it for the comedy. He said once the idea was developed, he would come in and play the coach.

"I knew he would make the number great; it needed Scott. Then everybody wanted to be in it, and pretty much the whole cast took part. That was a first."

The baseball number was a showstopper in 1991–92. It also provided the impetus for the wonderful, full-cast ensemble productions that would follow.

But it, too, was not without mishap.

In Toledo, Debi hurt her ankle during the show. She was on crutches and the baseball number was missing its big slugger.

Time for a pinch-hitter: Peter Carruthers.

"We kind of scrambled around, and I said, 'Sure I'll do it.' I just didn't want to kill somebody or run into anyone.

"I went out there, and I had never understudied her part, but I knew what the deal was—be funny. I tried to make it a spontaneous thing, not try to do what Debi would do, but be myself."

Carruthers was so good that when members of the audience learned it was not his regular part and that he was subbing for Debi, they were stunned.

The team. The family feeling. It is something that has branded Stars on Ice, from the early years until now, through triumph and tragedy.

"That was just an example of the group rallying and coming together to help the team," Peter said.

The team. The family feeling. It is something that has branded Stars on Ice, from the early years until now, through triumph and tragedy.

Everyone mentions it, from the skaters to the sponsors to the folks behind the scenes, making it all work. Making it all possible.

Kresge recalled the family effort it took to put together the "On the Town" number Scott originated.

"It had Scott, Michael Seibert, and Chris Harrison as the three sailors who spend their leave in New York, and Sandy Lenz, Lisa Carey, and Judy Blumberg were the women," Kresge said. "I cut the music and structured it into a 12-minute edited version. We began to choreograph it, then we had to do costumes.

"I can remember going to a local fabric store in a strip mall—these were the rude beginnings—then we had a former skating mom making the costumes. But somehow we got it on the boards, and this production number was one of the first ensemble pieces I can remember. And it worked because everyone pulled together to make it work."

She credits Scott with creating that togetherness at the very outset and never letting it falter.

SCOTT HAMILTON

Kresge recalled the family effort it took to put together the "On the Town" number Scott originated. . . . "When I think about Stars, always the constant is Scott and his never-ending enthusiasm and involvement and creativity. . . . I think he has done so much for the sport, too. And remained so human. . . ."

SCOTT HAMILTON, "MR. BOJANGLES"

"When I think about Stars, always the constant is Scott and his never-ending enthusiasm and involvement and creativity," Kresge said. "I think he has done so much for the sport, too. And remained so human. And given so much back and encouraged people and helped people."

Even when discord arose, as it often will in a family, particularly under the trying conditions the tour was dealing with in the early days, Scott smoothed the bumps, removed the hurdles.

DEBI THOMAS

Even when discord arose, as it often will in a family, particularly under the trying conditions the tour was dealing with in the early days, Scott smoothed the bumps, removed the hurdles.

At a rehearsal in Aspen before the 1991–92 season, Debi was struggling with the choreography in the finale, a Mardi Gras routine. She came late to a session in which the group was doing difficult splices between two lines.

Debi made several mistakes and, each time, would kick the ice.

"I said something like, 'Debi, grow up or get off the ice,'" Kresge recalled. "So she left the building and immediately called her manager. To me, that behavior was not acceptable."

1990–91 STARS ON ICE PROGRAM

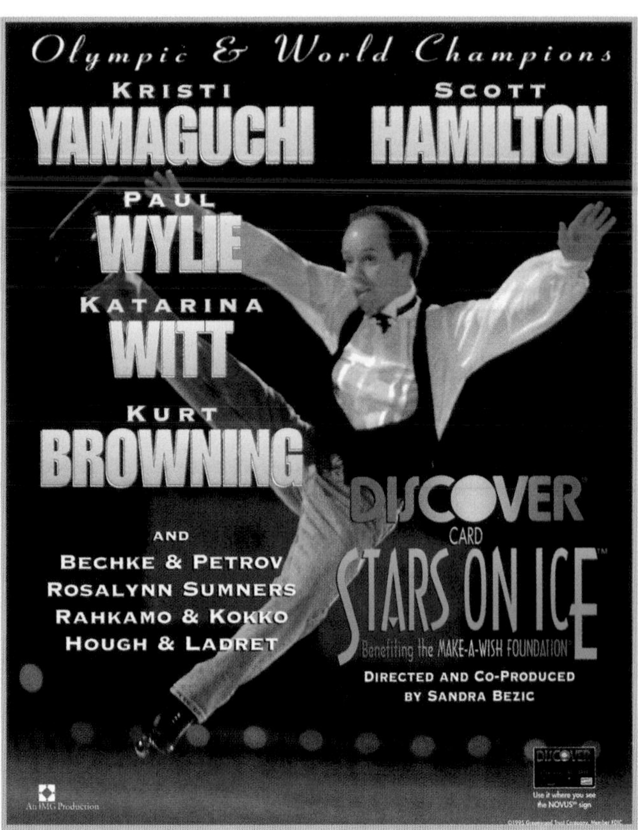

1995–96 STARS ON ICE POSTER

Incentives were devised for using Discover Card to purchase show tickets, with a portion of the price ($1 at the outset, then later $2) designated directly to the Make-A-Wish Foundation, which is the charity of record for Discover Card.

But Scott went to Debi and spoke with her and was able to patch it up. And the Mardi Gras number eventually meshed, with Debi having a key role in it. Debi ended up being a great source of inspiration that year, and in the end she was the most loved skater of that tour.

Rosalynn, the iron woman of the tour for not having missed even one show in the first dozen years, believes the humble roots of Stars on Ice brought everyone closer.

"It never became a grind," she said. "In the early days, it was like our own little thing, not like some big cover-of-*USA Today* story. We were so happy we were working and out there doing what we love to do and creating something."

IMG, meanwhile, was trying to create a place for Stars on Ice in the media, with sponsors, and with arenas.

Discover Card was so happy with its sponsorship that it asked for exclusivity, and was willing to pay for it. Swain told Chrysler of Discover's interest and Chrysler gave up its sponsorship of the U.S. tour.

Incentives were devised for using Discover Card to purchase show tickets, with a portion of the price ($1 at the outset, then later $2) designated directly to the Make-A-Wish Foundation, which is the charity of record for Discover Card.

The skaters would have Make-A-Wish days on which they would meet children who have serious or terminal illnesses, sometimes skate with them or have lunch together. Through the years, the association with Make-A-Wish would grow and, for as long as Scott can remember, it has been one of the highlights of the tour.

"We all look forward to those days, because the kids are so wonderful, so enthusiastic, and they keep you going," he said. "When they get on the ice and you see their eyes light up and how much fun they're having—there's nothing like that."

Television had become interested in Stars on Ice, too. ESPN had first televised the show in 1987, from Chicago, then came back again the next year. USA Network came aboard for 1989 and '90, followed by TNT in 1991.

By '92, two performances were being televised: TBS in December, right around or even on Christmas, and NBC in January, usually on the weekend preceding the Super Bowl, when there is no NFL on the tube.

The skaters would have Make-A-Wish days on which they would meet children who have serious or terminal illnesses, sometimes skate with them or have lunch. . . .

"Television was very important for several reasons," Swain explained. "It gave us the opportunity to show the product to large numbers. People saw the telecasts and appreciated the talent and the production. That inspired them to come and see the show live, and they would continue to come once they had seen it.

"And this show comes to life on television. As we progressed, we added new talent, but there was the comfort of not a lot of turnover, with the constants such as Scott and Rosalynn, and later Kristi and Paul.

"And, of course, there is a family atmosphere among all the skaters that clearly comes through."

"It is like a family," adds Karen Plage, Scott's longtime girlfriend. "The skaters spend more time together than with anyone else in their lives. Every day and night, so it's like a bunch of brothers and sisters. That attachment to each other creates a good working environment. They watch out for each other. They can tell if some-

(clockwise from left) YUKI SAEGUSA, MICHAEL SEIBERT, JUDY BLUMBERG, SCOTT HAMILTON, THREE SKATING CLUB HOSTESSES, LISA CAREY, CHRIS HARRISON, BRIAN POCKAR, ROSALYNN SUMNERS, SANDY LENZ, & TOLLER CRANSTON

> "I guess you could call it the backbone of Stars on Ice: We always felt like a family Maybe it was the way we grew up together in skating."

one is having some problems on the ice, and they know how to help."

Roz is a skater, and she more than anyone has grown with the show. Remember, she was its most reluctant member at first. Yet, through all the years, through cast changes and staff alterations, through triumph and tragedy, the one person whose blades always made it onto the ice was Rosalynn Sumners.

"I guess you could call it the backbone of Stars on Ice: we always felt like a family. Maybe it was the way we grew up together in skating. We had big histories that go a lot further than the tour. We competed with and against each other for years, on the way up in amateur skating, at nationals and worlds and the Olympics.

"Whenever a crisis happened, we would all stick together, because we had been through so much. Each thing brought us closer and closer. Together we accomplished what we did—accomplished some greatness—and are proud of it."

IMG was proud of what was developing, too. And it wanted to bring Stars on Ice to an even wider audience. So in March 1990, Canada became part of the schedule.

SCOTT HAMILTON & KURT BROWNING *(left)*
ROSALYNN SUMNERS *(right)*

Canadians are well-known for their love of the sport. Competitions throughout the years in the Dominion have sold out, particularly if they included the nation's big stars, from Toller Cranston to Brian Orser to Liz Manley to Kurt Browning to Elvis Stojko in singles. From Martini and Underhill to Wilson and McCall to Brasseur and Eisler to Bourne and Kraatz for pairs or dance.

But, again, the idea was to start small, in places like Peterborough and Kingston. Later on, the Montreal Forum and Molson Centre would be added. Or Maple Leaf Gardens and the Saddledome.

"All the aspects were in place for a tour in Canada," said Swain, "but we had to keep from getting ahead of ourselves in both the U.S. and Canada."

Stars on Ice in Canada would serve another, significant purpose in the figure skating world by becoming a testing ground for a new rule.

In 1991, Kurt Browning already was a two-time world champion and would head into the 1992 Olympics as a gold medal favorite. He was an IMG client, and here was Stars on Ice, bound for Canada and seeking a "homeboy" to headline the show—not all of the U.S. tour's performers would skate at the Canadian stops.

"Canada is a very educated skating market," said Michael Merrall, managing director for the Canadian tour. "But what is nearest and dearest to them is their own Canadian stars."

Having Browning and Orser at the top of the marquee seemed perfect. Except that Browning still had his Olympic eligibility, and by joining Stars, he could lose it.

KURT BROWNING, "ST. LOUIS BLUES"

Canadians are well-known for their love of the sport. Competitions throughout the years. . .have sold out, particularly if they included the nation's big stars, from Toller Cranston to Brian Orser to Liz Manley to Kurt Browning to Elvis Stojko in singles. From Martini and Underhill to Wilson and McCall to Brasseur and Eisler to Bourne and Kraatz for pairs or dance.

KITTY & PETER CARRUTHERS

TUFFY HOUGH & DOUG LADRET

BRIAN ORSER

SCOTT HAMILTON & BRIAN ORSER, "FIVE GUYS NAMED MOE"

"In the second year, we tried to be more ambitious," Merrall said. . . . "There was a wider offering of Canadian talent, and that was first and foremost for our portion of the tour."

IMG worked with the Canadian Figure Skating Association to create a vehicle for putting any money Kurt earned into a trust fund. Kurt became the first major amateur skater in Stars on Ice with that status, and it became a groundbreaking arrangement that skaters would take advantage of for years.

"Kurt was a special guest star in '91," recalled Merrall. "We brought the U.S. tour up to Canada, and with Kurt and Brian and Josée Chouinard, who was the top Canadian woman, it was a good solid corps."

"We wanted this to take off in Canada and grow to more cities," Brian said. "In the first year, we went into Vancouver, and Tracy, Rob, and myself would call the media ourselves and arrange interviews and send out press kits. I would use an alias and say I was with the tour and Tracy and Rob were available to talk about the tour, then Tracy would do the same for me. We had to try to get as much publicity for the show as we could. We were on a tight budget.

"From the beginning, I was kind of like the Scott Hamilton of the Canadian tour. Before we had Sandra Bezic, we were involved in a lot of the decisions on who would be in it and where they skated in the show. I was like a liaison between management and the skaters. They consulted me on stuff. That is pretty much Scott's role on the U.S. tour."

Brian always marveled at how most skating shows, and Stars on Ice in particular, received the same kind of attention in Canada that a rock tour might.

"The audiences would go crazy, give us a number of standing ovations," he said. "Not just for the Canadians. They just appreciated good skating, whether it was an American, or Russians or Torvill and Dean from England, or even some of the names not as well known.

"It is great to see the growth now. The great thing about being part of both tours is it started as a meat-and-potatoes tour, and look at what it has become."

Test shows for a second short stint in Canada were staged in Toronto, Vancouver, and Edmonton, and they played to half-filled buildings. Merrall called it a solid success but not overwhelming. Still, it created enough incentive for IMG to move ahead with a more substantial undertaking in early 1992.

"In the second year, we tried to be more ambitious," Merrall said. "Even though Kurt did not do as well as we hoped in the Olympics and did not medal, he kind of struck a chord with Canadians as a personality. Isabelle Brasseur and Lloyd Eisler were coming off bronze medals at the Olympics, and Christine "Tuffy" Hough and Doug Ladret were coming off a good showing. There was a wider offering of Canadian talent, and that was first and foremost for our portion of the tour.

"And it turned out a tremendous success in 10 cities."

By then, the U.S. tour had made some key changes.

For 1990–91, it had begun focusing on the first quarter of the year, with the

CHRISTINE "TUFFY" HOUGH & DOUG LADRET, "ARE YOU GONNA GO MY WAY?"

majority of stops scheduled between January 10 and April 7. Also, they were dropping some of the smaller cities: a Butte, Montana, for a St. Louis or Kansas City; a 4,000 to 6,000 seat arena for a 10,000 to 12,000 seater.

"We would sell out, but our costs of business had gotten much higher," Swain said of the smaller buildings. "Our overhead was growing rapidly and we needed to play in larger buildings where we could sell additional tickets since the opportunity was there."

Stars on Ice was slowly making headway. A solid portion of the schedule brought it to places such as Minneapolis, Pittsburgh, Detroit, Cleveland, Chicago, Miami, Cincinnati, Buffalo, Kansas City, and St. Louis. All major league towns with large arenas.

"At this point, the skaters wanted more," Swain said. "We had seen the Olympics come in 1988 and again in '92, and it was very positive and exciting to see in this four-year cycle we were still strong and continuing to grow, with the same talent."

Brian marveled, "The audiences would go crazy, give us a number of standing ovations. Not just for the Canadians. They just appreciated good skating, whether it was an American, or Russians or Torvill and Dean from England. . . ."

Stars on Ice was slowly making headway. . . ."We had seen the Olympics come in 1988 and again in '92, and it was very positive and exciting to see in this four-year cycle we were still strong and continuing to grow, with the same talent." But plagued by some of the old bugaboos.

But plagued by some of the old bugaboos.

In March of 1991, the tour stopped in Memphis. The Mid-South Coliseum hadn't hosted an ice show for a while.

Between the two groups of skater warmups, the zamboni driver was making ice, and the machine was spewing fumes throughout the building, giving off a terrible smell and lots of smoke.

Fortunately, much of the bad air went up into the dome-shaped ceiling of the Coliseum, but the second warmup was canceled after ten minutes because no one could breathe.

Building mechanics went to work on the zamboni as cast members went to dinner. The ice was cleaned for the show—despite more fumes—and Coliseum management cranked up the air conditioning to disperse the smell. The show went on as scheduled.

"But when the zamboni came out at the intermission following Act I, it did about three-quarters of a lap and died," Byron Allen recalled. "Right on the ice, even before it had a chance to asphyxiate the somewhat sparse crowd."

The zamboni driver tried unsuccessfully to restart it, then recruited a couple of stagehands to push it off the ice. After some slipping and sliding—but no budging—things began to look serious.

Would the show have a new prop for the second act?

"We asked around if anyone had a four-wheel drive vehicle which could tow the zamboni off the ice, and one of the stagehands came up with something along the lines of a Bronco," Allen said. "We hooked up a rope to the zamboni, the guy hit the gas, and the Bronco spun its wheels and went sideways. This was not going to work, either.

"At about that point, I looked at Kitty Carruthers and said, 'You and the other skaters may have to push it off.' She looked at me in disbelief."

After twenty minutes of searching, Allen found a security guard with a real truck, which was driven onto the ice and tied by rope to the zamboni.

"We finally pulled the beast off the ice, to much more than polite applause," he said with a laugh. "It was 45 minutes after the intermission started. A great deal of popcorn, sodas, and programs later, the rest of the show went on."

The variety in the show was growing, too. Production numbers ran the gamut, from the "Warsaw Concerto" to a Motown finale.

"That is one routine I remember, the 'Warsaw Concerto,'" Lea Ann said. "Karen and Billy and myself and Suzie Wynne and Joe Druar [former U.S. dance champions who were with the show for two seasons] felt we should have some classical music in the show.

"Karen found the 'Warsaw Concerto' and brought in the CD. We called it the

(clockwise from left) LEA ANN MILLER, BRIAN ORSER, TRACY WILSON, & ROSALYNN SUMNERS, "MOCK ME AMADEUS"

'War Zone Concerto.' We hated the costumes—peach and turquoise, I recall—and rolled our eyes every night when we had to wear them. It was one of those things we just should have left alone."

Leaving things alone never has been the style for Stars on Ice. So with the Albertville Games at hand, IMG did more experimenting.

The opener for 1991–92 was in Denver on November 21, and it was taped for television. The bulk of the tour was in the first quarter of 1992, the prime dates long sought. But on January 28, after the show in Roanoke, Virginia, Stars stopped. For a month.

The variety in the show was growing, too. Production numbers ran the gamut, from the "Warsaw Concerto" to a Motown finale.

KRISTI YAMAGUCHI, "JULIET"

"I don't think we ever considered touring during the Olympics," Swain said. "It was an easy decision at that time.

"We always looked at it as a positive, the Olympic exposure, particularly with Scott doing the TV for CBS at the Games. That always focused people's attention on skating, with new stars coming into the spotlight and Scott talking about them to a huge audience.

"When we returned to the tour, the Olympics always were like a shot in the arm. It was a plus and remains a plus for us. Just look at the amount of time figure skating receives in telecasts and look at the ratings numbers. I don't believe any other sport commands the amount of time or the numbers."

Albertville created two very big American stars: gold medalist Kristi Yamaguchi and silver medalist Paul Wylie. Just as in 1988 after Calgary, IMG understood the need to grab the headliners. In the tradition that the show was establishing, these major players in skating would be blended right into the family.

"From Day One, when they first called it Stars on Ice, it either sank or swam with everyone," Lea Ann said. "We all do well and the show is great, and that is what a tour and a family is all about. You want everyone to be successful and happy.

"Figure skating can be such a selfish sport, an all-about-me sport. But it was all about us in the early years and about making this idea work.

"That was the foundation for what Stars on Ice would become."

PAUL WYLIE, "IT'S A GUY GIRL THING"

Albertville created two very big American stars: gold medalist Kristi Yamaguchi and silver medalist Paul Wylie. Just as in 1988 after Calgary, IMG understood the need to grab the headliners.

✯ CHAPTER THREE

THE MASTERPIECES

"What Stars on Ice needed was a single direction. My mission was very clear: to direct these really wonderfully talented skaters, and to give them a place and production level where they could shine."

Sandra Bezic—director, co-producer

By 1992, IMG was a major player in figure skating. Having signed Brian Orser and Debi Thomas after the Calgary Olympics, then getting Ekaterina Gordeeva and Sergei Grinkov in 1991, the talent base had been expanded.

Discover Card was thrilled with the response it was getting from sponsoring Stars on Ice. Television was happy with the ratings. Now it was time to take the steps that would solidify the show for the rest of the decade.

First and foremost was adding more stars. Bob Kain, having missed out on Calgary gold medalists Brian Boitano and Katarina Witt, who established their own tour, knew he had to get at least one of the Albertville winners. And he knew which one: Kristi Yamaguchi.

After Calgary, Kain and IMG had hoped that Debi Thomas would be a long-term star, but, as Gary Swain explained, "There was a lot Debi needed to learn about show skating." When she fell, for example, she got upset—despite Scott's insistence on keeping the right attitude with the crowd.

"Debi struggled with that," according to Swain. "She also had a lot of things going on with her schooling. She wanted to be much more than a skater, and we

SCOTT HAMILTON & KRISTI YAMAGUCHI, "SHAMELESS"

At the heart of constant growth has been,

naturally, the talent.

"Everything that happened in '92 was more than I had dreamed of," said Kristi, "winning the U.S. title for the first time and then doing so well at the Olympics and coming back to Oakland and defending my world title. It seemed to wrap things up so perfectly. I couldn't help thinking, 'How could I top that?'"

all applauded her for it. I think it was a little tough for her to focus."

As Kain put it, "Debi didn't stay long, but got us to the '92 Olympics," and now there were the stars of Albertville to consider. Kristi and Paul Wylie were, by far, the most attractive.

Kristi was waffling about what to do. She was only 21 when she won at Albertville, far outdistancing a field that included Midori Ito, one of her idols, and Nancy Kerrigan, who won silver and bronze. In a way, there were no more worlds to conquer in Olympic-eligible skating.

"Everything that happened in '92 was more than I had dreamed of," said Kristi, "winning the U.S. title for the first time and then doing so well at the Olympics and coming back to Oakland and defending my world title. It seemed to wrap things up so perfectly. I couldn't help thinking, 'How could I top that?'"

Kain was thinking the same way—how could she top such a hat trick?

"We wanted her to be the new star to go with our established stars, so it was not a hard choice for us."

But Kristi had to make a choice: which tour? That's where Sandra Bezic's role became critical.

IMG bought out the Boitano-Witt tour that year, which made Bezic, who had already done choreography for Kristi, available to work with Stars on Ice.

Kain knew that bringing Bezic aboard could sway Kristi toward joining Stars on Ice. Also Bezic would bring to Stars on Ice the same production value that the Boitano-Witt tour had enjoyed.

"Kristi felt most comfortable with Sandra," Kain said, "but even though she had won the gold medal and had the clout, Kristi never demanded that Sandra do the show; she never insisted that Sandra be director or main choreographer."

That was not exactly the way Karen Kresge, the show's director from its humble beginning through the 1991–92 season, heard it.

"Stars was looking to acquire new talent," she said

with the slighest trace of bitterness. "Kristi had done a lot of work with Sandra, and I knew when the two shows merged that they were going to have to choose. The unofficial word was Kristi said she wouldn't come unless Sandra came, and Sandra said it would not work unless she was [in charge] with her own people.

"Sandra does great work for Stars on Ice," Karen added graciously, "and she has done so for years."

Bezic admitted having Kristi in her corner didn't hurt.

Kain said hiring Bezic was "the right next step. She would be the leader. That was the easy one."

Bezic understood that it was time for Stars on Ice to make an everlasting mark in figure skating and show business. At the same time, she didn't want to upset too many of the established patterns.

"What I saw was a whole bunch of people who are extremely creative, all offering up suggestions, trying to tie things up themselves, which is really difficult for performers to do. What Stars on Ice needed was a single direction. My mission was very clear: to direct these really wonderfully talented skaters, and to give them a place and production level where they could shine."

SANDRA BEZIC

It would be costly. IMG understood that.

"Sandra really brought things to a whole new level," Swain said. "Her team, with Michael Seibert as her co-director and Lea Ann Miller, knew how to go about reaching that level. With her presentation, we were as confident to go into, say, a Madison Square Garden in New York as into any other market."

But long before the tour would hit the meccas of entertainment and sports, Bezic had to develop a feel for her new charges.

"We needed to build a relationship. I needed to show they could trust me."

So Bezic called a production meeting in Vail, where she interviewed all of the skaters individually and also as a group to find out what they had in mind for the show. For two days the skaters talked, and Bezic recorded the discussions. When she listened to the tapes, it helped her key into exactly where the skaters thought the show was and where they wanted it to go.

"I knew who they were and how they skated. But I wanted to bring to them the understanding of the power of the group. Up to that point, they were individual stars appearing in a collective presentation. I wanted them to know how wonderful it could feel to move forward together. I took baby steps in that direction."

Where she took giant steps was in the hiring of personnel and enhancing the production values for Stars on Ice. There would be no compromising here.

"I really threw a lot at IMG," she said, "and they totally supported me. They

"My mission was very clear: to direct these really wonderfully talented skaters, and to give them a place and production level where they could shine. . . . We needed to build a relationship. . . . I knew who they were and how they skated. But I wanted to bring to them the understanding of the power of the group."

SCOTT HAMILTON & PAUL WYLIE, "JUMP"

"Every night we go out, we do a show and we entertain the crowd. That is very different from being sort of locked up for six months in your ice rink training for one night or two nights of competition."

allowed me to do my job and didn't try to second-guess me."

They also supported her entire production crew, headed by Seibert. In fact, once the show hit the road, Bezic would make only occasional trips to see it, leaving that role to Seibert.

While Stars on Ice was making these huge changes behind the scenes, the cast was also undergoing a significant makeover. Debi left and Kristi came aboard. Lea Ann Miller joined Bezic's staff and Bill Fauver retired. Ice dancers Suzie Wynne and Joe Druar left, replaced by Canadian pair Tuffy Hough and Doug Ladret.

"The end for me was difficult," said Fauver, now a skating teacher in Nashville. "For every athlete, the door begins to shut at some time. It's not that you aren't physically able. Sometimes your life changes.

"I enjoyed touring and still miss it and the crowds," Fauver added, but in his case, change came in the form of marriage and a family.

Also joining Stars on Ice was Paul Wylie. Although he didn't win gold at Albertville, Paul staged the performance of his life in the Olympics to finish second to Viktor Petrenko. In fact, Paul was considered the third man on that U.S. Olympic team, behind Christopher Bowman and Todd Eldredge.

Instead, the old man—he was 27 at the time and a magna cum laude graduate of Harvard—nearly became the best man.

"The problem was I had never won a national championship, even though I had been in 12 senior nationals," Paul said. "They called me a 'practice skater,' because they thought I skated well in practice, but folded under pressure.

"But when I skated in Albertville, and had the night of my life under the biggest pressure of my life, I answered all my critics. Whatever happened before the Olympics, the Albertville experience completely eradicated. It sent me to a whole new level, even in the way I see myself. It was kind of a magical weekend."

A weekend that placed him in much demand as he turned pro. After he soared above the critics and the competition at the Olympics, Paul looked around for a place to "enhance my skating" before heading off for law school or business school.

He didn't have to look very far.

"I think Stars on Ice was a natural fit for me," he said. "I love the fact it is a package, almost like playing for a team. Every night we go out, we do a show and we entertain the crowd. That is very different from being sort of locked up for six months in your ice rink training for one night or two nights of competition.

"We can choose a piece of music and interpret it however we want. We don't have to do four different spins in our program. We don't have to pack it with too many triples so you can't interpret the work as music."

When the bolstered cast and new production crew gathered in Lake Placid, there were some nerves, as there always are for opening night. But underneath, there was a flowing current of confidence. And of expectation.

"Sort of like reaching for new horizons," Scott said. "That's always what we wanted this tour to be about, anyway."

Bezic felt she immediately got the trust of the skaters that she sought. But she didn't believe they realized until that opening night just what they had created together.

"Then the show was so well-received, and they were so excited about it," she said. "They told me individually what they felt we had. They acknowledged the fact we made a good team." The new team had new goals. Higher goals. The profile of Stars on Ice would change forever.

"We had bought out the Boitano-Witt tour from Bill Graham Presents and we got Kristi and Paul," Kain said. "As we went into 1992–93, the jet engine started

"They called me a 'practice skater,' because they thought I skated well in practice, but folded under pressure. But when I skated in Albertville, and had the night of my life under the biggest pressure of my life, I answered all my critics."

KURT BROWNING, "ALL ALONE"

GORDEEVA & GRINKOV, "IT'S A GUY GIRL THING"

BECHKE & PETROV, "SAMSON & DELILAH"

cooking. That was when we became THE winter tour, solid forever, and we could say we had made it. It worked perfectly."

And it worked everywhere. In the smaller markets, fans were seeing things they normally would have to travel to Broadway to see. One of Bezic's strengths was making it all play well in those towns as well as the big cities. Stars on Ice was versatile enough to play anywhere, with a broad selection of music that appealed to everybody.

The show opened in Lake Placid, which quickly was becoming a home away from home for the troupe. Bezic and company had developed several numbers that would become signature routines for some skaters.

Scott came up with a smooth, totally relaxing showcase for Frank Sinatra's "Someone to Watch Over Me." Paul's first solo for the show was to the powerful soundtrack of the film "JFK." The two of them put on a rollicking performance together doing "Jump."

Kristi found just the right vehicle in "Wishing on a Star," then followed with En Vogue's "My Lovin'," which displayed all of the sexy charm she never dared to put across as an Olympic-eligible competitor.

"It was kind of a break for me from what I had been doing," she said. "But that's why I was in the show in the first place—to have that kind of opportunity."

Hough and Ladret performed a sizzling "Story of the Blues."

"I always wanted to perform in the show," Hough said, "and at the same time have the freedom to be myself. Stars was the only show that gave Doug and myself opportunities beyond our dreams."

"Sandra deserved much of the credit. She is the one person who pulled it all together, taking the talents and egos and making it work . . . .Sandra gave us a lot of depth."

The finale was a memorable tribute to Queen, from "We Will Rock You" to "Crazy Little Thing Called Love" to "The Show Must Go On."

And from the classically trained Katia and Sergei to the funkiness of Gary Beacom, it worked.

Perhaps better than anyone imagined it would.

"We were big time," said Swain. "The quality and variety of skating, the depth from classical to rock, fast to slow, with singles, pairs, dance, the group ensembles —the full package was there.

"Sandra deserved much of the credit. She is the one person who pulled it all together, taking the talents and egos and making it work. She seems to have a knack for knowing how to best present a skater, how to challenge them and play off their strengths. Sandra gave us a lot of depth."

So much so that Stars on Ice was ready for any challenge. Nobody realized that more than Scott.

When the show's first appearance at Madison Square Garden was booked for the winter of 1993, Scott's first thought was, "'About time!' But I also knew we were ready."

KRISTI YAMAGUCHI, "MY LOVIN'"

PAUL WYLIE, "JFK"

KRISTI & DOUG IN REHEARSAL FOR "IT'S A GUY GIRL THING"

Ultimate validation for Stars on Ice came on the night of February 19.

"The standards are so high for entertainment there," Swain said. "It was not just another step in credibility, it was a huge step. A kind of a sign to the skaters of reaching the pinnacle.

"In those first few years," Swain continued, "there were times we never really knew if we would make it to a Madison Square Garden. But once we went there and were such a hit, we knew we'd be able to come back every year. We knew the sky was the limit."

Years earlier, the International Olympic Committee decided to separate the Summer Olympics and Winter Olympics. That meant putting either a two-year or six-year span between Winter Games, and the IOC opted to have a Winter Olympics in Lillehammer, Norway, two years after the Albertville Games.

So Kristi and Paul had been with Stars on Ice for one season when another Olympics appeared on the horizon. This one came with an enormous difference: professionals were allowed back to compete.

Katia and Sergei decided to regain their eligibility, go back to Russia, and train for Lillehammer. They were replaced by Russian ice dancers Natalia Annenko and Genrikh Sretenski.

Scott also recaptured his eligibility, but he wasn't going anywhere.

"My special time was in 1984. Those were my Olympics. Now, it's time for others to have their spot in the limelight.

"Besides," he added with a smile, "I'll be in the CBS booth, so I'll be there."

Paul never even considered going back.

"Why?" he said. "My last performance on that level was when I won the silver medal [at Albertville]. That's how I want it to be."

Kristi faced a more difficult decision. She was in her prime, just two years removed from winning gold. And there really wasn't anyone—Kerrigan, Tonya Harding, Oksana Baiul—who figured to challenge her if she returned.

At first, she thought about going back in the pairs; Kristi won two U.S. championships partnered with Rudy Galindo, and she admitted that the pairs was the one part of the sport she really missed.

Kristi faced a more difficult decision. She was in her prime, just two years removed from winning gold. . . . "If I could find a partner. . . ."

"The Olympics are something I will always look back on and remember with a smile. I knew it was time to go on."

"If I could find a partner . . ." she added with a giggle.

But when she evaluated where her current life was—and where she had been—well, Kristi wanted to stay right where she was. That meant with Stars on Ice.

"The Olympics are something I will always look back on and remember with a smile. I knew it was time to go on."

Kristi had grown considerably as an artist in her first year with the tour. But she also grew in another way. She accepted the role of spokeswoman—for herself, for figure skating, for Stars on Ice.

That role was not comfortable for her at the outset.

"It's not that she was ever reticent about doing interviews," said tour publicist Lynn Plage. "But during her years as an amateur—for instance in 1989 at the nationals in Baltimore—her interviews were painful. We convinced the USFSA to get media training for the skaters.

"But I saw the first year she was with Stars on Ice that she is an excellent listener, and I knew she would improve. And she wants to do it all."

In that first year, Kristi did a dozen media days, and, according to Plage, became adept at listening to the questions, as well as observing how Scott and Paul and other skaters handled the media. Gradually she became much more confident in her ability.

"We would talk about the Kristi inside," Plage continued. "I wanted her to see that people wanted to know about her. It takes at least a year following their amateur days, where they are so coddled, to come into their own. She definitely came into her own."

The 1993–94 tour would be broken up by the Lillehammer Games. Some of the key stars were off doing television commentaries—Paul and Scott with CBS and Brian Orser working for Canadian television. Kristi would do radio analysis. Roz would work for TNT in Atlanta.

So after the Lake Placid debut on Thanksgiving weekend, followed by a break for the holidays, the real tour started the day after Christmas in Seattle. It would go through February 3, 1994, in Orlando, then take a month off for the Olympics before resuming.

The Canadian tour also would be in full swing for April. The momentum from the 1992–93 season hadn't ebbed.

"It had been a pivotal and exciting year," Swain said. "We realized we could continue to grow and look at expanding to other continents, and we realized we could sell out arenas. The sponsors were very happy with the results, and we felt we could keep Discover Card for a long period of time."

But Bob Kain, for one, was worried about the prospect of another Olympics so soon. He had plucked the stars from '92 and had hoped they would have a four-year run.

"I would have liked to have another Olympics in 1990, when we didn't get the gold-medal winners from '88, but after '92, I would have preferred another Olympics in six years, not two."

Five members of the cast—instead of looking ahead to the next Olympics—wanted to look back ten years to their Olympics, in Sarajevo in '84. Yes, they had their wonderful memories, but the reality of what happened during the Yugoslav civil war made Scott, Brian, Rosalynn, Kitty, and Peter want to pay homage to their special city.

So they worked with the choreographers—two of whom, Michael Seibert and Lea Ann Miller, also competed in the '84 Games—on a number set to Elton John's "Funeral for a Friend" and Bette Midler's rendition of the Beatles' "In My Life."

"The people there gave us so much," Scott said. "We wanted to do something to acknowledge those people. They are going through really rough times. The war is not something that will go away, but it's devastating to see that city turned into a killing ground."

Bringing the tribute to fruition was Bezic's job. Her heritage is Eastern European,

Five members of the cast—instead of looking ahead to the next Olympics—wanted to look back ten years to their Olympics, in Sarajevo in '84.

BRIAN ORSER, KITTY CARRUTHERS, SCOTT HAMILTON, PETER CARRUTHERS, & ROSALYNN SUMNERS, THE "SARAJEVO TRIBUTE" PERFORMANCE

(clockwise from left) HOUGH & LADRET, "ARE YOU GONNA GO MY WAY?"; SCOTT, "WALK THIS WAY"; & ROSALYNN IN A DONNA SUMMERS ANTHOLOGY

and she thought with the ten-year anniversary and seven people whose lives were touched—and remained touched—by Sarajevo, it was the right thing to do.

Each skater wore a different color from the Olympic flag. They performed alone and as a group. Each performance brought a groundswell of emotions for every one of them.

"It's powerful music, powerful emotions, powerful memories," said Rosalynn, who won a silver medal in those Games.

Added Lea Ann, "It's almost like having an extended reunion."

Lea Ann remembered walking into the packed stadium for opening ceremonies and spotting her grandfather in the stands. He was the person who got her started in skating.

"The venue where I had that moment," she said solemnly, shaking her head, "it's a graveyard."

"The number is hard to do in many ways, because we remember Sarajevo as the most wonderful time of our lives," Scott said. "The city was so festive, beautiful. The entire country sacrificed to put on those games. Now the buildings that hosted some of the most memorable and beautiful performances in athletic history are being used as morgues and bomb shelters. If they are standing at all."

Their need to recapture the feeling of joy and peace of 1984—not only for themselves, but for the audience, and for the future—spurred the Sarajevo veterans to action.

"It was a different Sarajevo then," said Kitty. "There was a picture of the arena in *Time* magazine, and the scoreboard was dangling. The first thing I think of is that I'll never be able to show my children that place and let them experience it the way I did."

The Sarajevo tribute was the highlight of another diverse program that included a solid string of rock 'n' roll featuring Rosalynn doing a Donna Summers anthology; Tuffy and Doug going wild to Lenny Kravitz's "Are You Gonna Go My Way?"; and Scott's soon-to-be-classic "Walk This Way" by Aerosmith.

Not to mention the other Scott classic that came out of that year: his tribute to lounge lizards in "I Love Me."

"I can't say there was any year I enjoyed doing my numbers more than that year," he admitted.

Paul was as cool as Chicago in the Roaring Twenties as he cavorted through "The Untouchables." Rosalynn was dreamy in "Smoke Gets in Your Eyes." Brian was coyly comical with "Deeply Dippy" and casually charming to Van Morrison's "Moondance."

The far-ranging finale went from Barry White to Perry Como, from Madonna to the Manhattan Transfer, from Duke Ellington to Janet Jackson.

As good as the program was, however, it could never grab the headlines once

The Sarajevo tribute was the highlight of another diverse program that included a solid string of rock 'n' roll featuring Rosalynn doing a Donna Summers anthology; Tuffy and Doug going wild to Lenny Kravitz's "Are You Gonna Go My Way?"; and Scott's soon-to-be-classic "Walk This Way" by Aerosmith.

the saga of Tonya and Nancy hit the airwaves. Everywhere Stars on Ice stopped, the skaters were asked as much about the Harding-Kerrigan mess as about the show.

For the most part, they kindly demurred from commenting on the attack on Kerrigan at nationals and the subsequent investigation into Harding's then-husband and the band of accomplices who planned and executed the knee-bashing.

And while all of the cast members were stunned by such developments, they were even more shocked at how it brought figure skating into a new, more glaring spotlight. One that has yet to dim.

Kristi had competed against Kerrigan and Harding for several years. In 1991, when Kristi was a strong favorite to win her first U.S. title, Harding upset her at Minneapolis—in the process becoming the first American woman and second in the world behind Midori Ito of Japan to hit a triple axel. No other woman had done it.

Kristi and Kerrigan were friends. They finished 1-3 at Albertville, where Harding was fourth.

"Because this is such an isolated incident, we don't feel it's going to happen to every other skater out there," said Kristi. "But skaters on the tour are literally two feet from the stands, so you have to put a lot of faith in the audience."

Paul and Kerrigan had the same coaches throughout their competitive careers. They had grown close, even doing a duet in various exhibitions.

"It hurt badly to see Nancy in such pain at what is supposed to be the height of her career," he said. "This is completely out of the realm of what you'd expect in figure skating."

BRIAN ORSER, "MOONDANCE"

The far-ranging finale went from Barry White to Perry Como, from Madonna to the Manhattan Transfer, from Duke Ellington to Janet Jackson.

Back in '94 . . . Scott was left to wonder just where Stars on Ice fit in this figure skating upheaval.

But figure skating would benefit in unexpected ways from the tale of conspiracy amid the so-called glamour. As would Stars on Ice.

As Scott sat in the CBS broadcast booth at the figure skating facility in Hamar, Norway, he couldn't help but laugh. While he was chatting in a near-empty arena, the practice rink next door was filled beyond capacity. Television crews, photographers, and reporters were cramped together in the tiny building while Tonya and Nancy went through their first practice session on the same ice.

Of course, the whole soap opera had gotten out of hand. But, wise man and savvy entrepreneur that he is, Scott knew the face of figure skating had changed forever. He also knew that Stars on Ice would be affected.

"I don't think there is any question that things are going to be different for everyone in skating," he said, and he was absolutely right.

KATARINA WITT, "SCHINDLER'S LIST"

Since 1994, the skating world has undergone an almost incomprehensible alteration. Television is overrun by competitions, specials, and exhibitions. From early fall until mid-spring, it's virtually impossible not to find skating programming on the air.

Back in '94, however, Scott was left to wonder just where Stars on Ice fit in this figure skating upheaval. Would it be damaged by the sordidness of Tonya-Nancy? Would it be helped by the wave of attention directed toward the sport?

Would not having either of the characters from that saga as part of the show hurt? Or would it be a benefit to be far removed from the fray?

Kain, meanwhile, was too busy going after the Lillehammer talent to deal with such questions. His primary target was Katarina, who only a few years earlier was a centerpiece in the only tour that really ever challenged Stars on Ice.

"Who wouldn't want Katarina?" he said. "She's a two-time Olympic champion who came from the mysterious East Germany and has become a star in the West.

"Kat also has an aura. She's sexy and she's athletic and she's artistic and she

Kain, meanwhile, was too busy going after the Lillehammer talent to deal with such questions. His primary target was Katarina, who only a few years earlier was a centerpiece in the only tour that really ever challenged Stars on Ice.

"Who wouldn't want Katarina?. . . She's a two-time Olympic champion who came from the mysterious East Germany and has become a star in the West. Kat also has an aura. She's sexy and she's athletic and she's artistic and she plays so well to the audience. Of course we wanted to sign her." Which IMG did, almost immediately bringing her aboard Stars on Ice.

KATARINA WITT, "SUMMERTIME"

plays so well to the audience. Of course we wanted to sign her."

Which IMG did, almost immediately bringing her aboard Stars on Ice.

Another target was Kurt Browning. The only question was, since Kurt had never won an Olympic medal, would he stick around for Nagano in 1998? It was a question he was ready to answer.

"Actually, I wanted to turn pro when Kristi turned pro, but my Olympics [in '92] did not go as well, and I decided to stay with the amateurs for another two years. This time, I felt ready."

Another target was Kurt Browning. The only question was, since Kurt had never won an Olympic medal, would he stick around for Nagano in 1998?. . ."Actually, I wanted to turn pro when Kristi turned pro, but my Olympics (in '92) did not go as well, and I decided to stay with the amateurs for another two years. This time, I felt ready."

So were Kain and IMG, who wanted to unveil the new talent right away. There was just too much momentum from Lillehammer, and keeping such potentially strong draws as Katarina and Kurt on the sidelines until the following winter made no sense.

"That Olympics had so much focus and such high ratings and people went so crazy," Kain said. "At first, we figured we would do the cities in Canada with Kurt, but then we had a better idea. We said, 'You know what, we're going to the Garden, why not dazzle New York?'"

They did not publicize the appearances by Katarina and Kurt. Their names were omitted from the program, and the existing cast kept the secret during media day.

"New York is a good place to have a surprise," Kain said.

Neither of them skated in the introductions. Then, early in the first act, the announcer said, simply, "Please welcome guest star Kurt Browning."

And there was Kurt, as Humphrey Bogart's Rick from "Casablanca."

Shortly thereafter came the second surprise introduction, for Katarina. And there she was, with her routine to "Where Have All the Flowers Gone?"

"It was really a cool moment," Kain said. "When Katarina came on, it was the loudest ovation we got. That was a good way for them to become a part of Stars on Ice."

Already a big part of Stars on Ice were the Make-A-Wish days. The plight of these disabled children could be wearing on the performers. But the spirit and the sheer joy the kids displayed was so uplifting that the skaters eagerly looked forward to those days.

If the kids couldn't skate, Scott would push them around the ice while they sat on chairs. Or the skaters might even carry a child around.

"I know what they are going through," Scott said. "It's scary when you're a little kid. It's nice for them to play hooky and get away from the hospitals and the loneliness."

At one of the days, in Kansas City, Kristi convinced Toronto Blue Jays outfielder Joe Carter—a recent World Series hero—to join her. The fact that Carter had been on the ice just once in his life didn't faze Kristi.

"He's an athlete. He won't have any problems," she said.

EKATERINA GORDEEVA &
KURT BROWNING, "FEVER"

"I'm not a pitcher," Carter added. "Pitching is all they can do."

Carter did just fine, leading some kids around the ice as Michael Bolton music played in the background and even trying to slap some hockey pucks into an empty net. But when one of his errant shots struck a cameraman—no injuries were reported—he gave that up.

"I want all these kids to dream and believe that the dream can come true," Carter said.

Added Kristi, for whom the Make-a-Wish days have been extra special, "I love children and I love to give something back to them."

The following season marked the return of G&G, meaning the 1994–95 cast featured a total of six Olympic gold medals.

Katia and Sergei returned with a new daughter, Daria, which made for some scrambling by the Russian champions. But Kurt faced the biggest adjustment. Already a superstar in Canada, where IMG planned to have him headline Stars on Ice Canada, he was much less familiar to American audiences.

"There is an even-level quality to Stars on Ice. We definitely have our superstars, but they don't make any of us feel like a supporting cast."

"I felt I had to introduce myself to the audience in the U.S.," he said. "All the skaters on tour had earned their spot in Stars on Ice. I felt I had to do that, too.

"There is an even-level quality to Stars on Ice. We definitely have our superstars, but they don't make any of us feel like a supporting cast. And Sandra has her way of making each skater look his or her best, so I felt at home with the rest of the cast right away. But my relationship to the audience in the U.S. is what has changed the most for me.

"Hey, now, I can't tell if I am in the U.S. or Canada."

In retrospect, the most endearing and ironic number on the 1994-95 program was G&G's "The Man I Love."

For power, Paul's "Schindler's List," followed by Katarina skating to the same music was almost overwhelming.

KURT BROWNING, "SERENADE TO SONIA"

GORDEEVA & GRINKOV, "THE MAN I LOVE"

Scott was suave and sophisticated to Tony Bennett's "Steppin' Out." And he brought down the house every night with an outlandish costume and outrageous footwork to "Cuban Pete."

"One thing we really got into was the finale, featuring the Stones," Scott said. "It was something I had thought about for awhile, and Sandra and everybody really brought it together. I don't know if anyone had skated to a whole bunch of Stones songs before. I doubt it."

Seibert's strongest memory of the performance list from that year was "Five Minutes for Icing," a stomping number in which the skates actually were miked.

"I think we were reaching new heights every year," Seibert said.

It was a great season, a great time for Stars on Ice.

The following season marked the return of G&G, meaning the 1994–95 cast featured a total of six Olympic gold medals. . . .Katia and Sergei returned with a new daughter, Daria. . . .

GORDEEVA & GRINKOV, "VOCALISE"   SUSANNA RAHKAMO & PETRI KOKKO, "THE PSALM"

NATALIA ANNENKO & GENRIKH SRETENSKI,
"PRAYER FOR THE DYING"

RADKA KOVARIKOVA & RENE NOVOTNY, "STILL IN LOVE"

"We tried to patch it together," Bezic said. "Obviously, there were some holes that could never be filled."

No one could have foreseen the tragedy that lay just a few months ahead.

Heading into 1995–96, the only significant cast change was the replacement of Annenko and Sretenski by Finnish ice dancers Susanna Rahkamo and Petri Kokko.

But during the week of final rehearsals, the unthinkable occurred: Sergei Grinkov collapsed on the ice and died of a massive heart attack. (The full story of this shattering event, and its profound effect upon Stars on Ice, will be unfolded in Chapter Five.)

As Bezic said, "That is when we became a family that nothing could tear apart. It was one of those lessons that brought us all back to earth and made us thankful for what we had and reminded us to cherish it."

To Bezic, it no longer mattered when the tour began. "We were supposed to open that week, and I remember at the meeting we had the next night someone was trying to push us into doing it. You know, 'The show must go on.' It was someone outside the company, and I looked up and said, 'NO. THE SHOW MUST NOT GO ON. This is a death, not a broken leg.'"

When the cast members reassembled ten days later to get the tour started, they worked at a slower pace. When someone had to go stand in a corner and cry, he did. When people had to sit out a portion of a rehearsal to gather themselves, they did.

But these are true professionals, and one thing they wanted most was to keep at it, keep making Stars on Ice better, keep making themselves better.

And, by keeping Sergei in mind, they were able to do that.

"We tried to patch it together," Bezic said. "Obviously, there were some holes that could never be filled."

Still, there was an entire schedule to fulfill, and the troupe had assembled a superb set of routines that included a Spaghetti Western; Paul's "Apollo 13," which would become a trademark number for him; Rosalynn's touching "Remember Me This Way"; Kurt's rousing "Brick House," with which he would win two world professional championships; Elena and Denis in a passionate performance about lost love, "Love To Spartacus"; and Scott—yes, the balding Scott—doing "Hair."

To finish off the evening, the cast skated to tunes by the Beatles and John Lennon solos. And when they performed to "Imagine," or "Starting Over," who couldn't think of Katia?

When a tribute show to Sergei—"A Celebration of a Life"—was being planned, Bezic was asked to contribute.

"It was really great," Bezic recalled,

RENÉE ROCA & GORSHA SUR, "TIME TO SAY GOODBYE"

KATIA, DARIA, & SERGEI

"It's hard to hang up your skates . . . I know that it's never going to be the same without Sergei, but I can still improve and still learn."

"because it gave us a sense of purpose. We would do the show for Katia and [daughter] Dasha, but it never occurred to us Katia would skate.

"When she said she would, we were in shock. How could she? Then it occurred to me . . . of course, she has to."

Bezic flew to Ottawa, where Katia and Marina Zoueva, her choreographer and close friend, were working on a number that would close the first act of the special show in Hartford on February 27. Bezic told Katia she would take all her directives from her, that this was Katia's show.

"I was devastated, seeing her skating alone," Bezic said. "It took my breath away. But she was truly happy, and it made so much sense. We proceeded to make a show which was very special—and it was all at Katia's request. There wasn't a skater in the world who didn't want to be there. It was based on what she thought would make him happy, knowing that he was watching."

No show, no competition, no Olympics, ever was so heart-wrenching or nerve-shattering for Bezic.

"In one moment, I'm having to worry about making sure it goes right, working at it," she said. "And in the next moment I'm sobbing, with tears running down my face. It was without a doubt one of the most emotional, maybe the most emotional night of my entire work life."

But that's what Stars on Ice is all about. Making it work, making it fun, making it meaningful, and making it all like family. As great as its participation list has been through the years, Stars on Ice in a way became STARS ON ICE in 1996.

The most heartwarming story was Katia's return, as a soloist. Buoyed by the acceptance of the audience for her singles work, and encouraged by everyone in the cast to come back, Katia rejoined the tour full time.

"It's hard to hang up your skates," she said. "I know that it's never going to be the same without Sergei, but I can still improve and still learn."

New to the cast were 1995 world pairs champions Radka Kovarikova and Rene Novotny—replacing Tuffy and Doug, who retired. Jill Trenary, a two-time U.S. champion, also came aboard.

EKATERINA GORDEEVA, "A CELEBRATION OF A LIFE"

And, oh yes: Torvill and Dean.

Perhaps the most creative and awe-inspiring couple in skating history, the authors of "Bolero"—the most memorable single performance at the 1984 Olympics (and possibly any other)—were a most welcome addition to the tour.

They had been starring in their own tours, and the burden of carrying the whole show had drained them.

"If we weren't fit or healthy," Christopher explained, "that show doesn't go on, and somebody gets upset, whether it's the public or the financers. It's refreshing not to have to feel that responsibility now. All the skaters here are headliners in their own right."

And oh yes, Torvill and Dean. . . ."They bring a lot of class, creativity, and experience. . . .They also bring a whole other audience. . . ."

"To be in this company is pretty special," Jayne added.

T&D's influence was apparent throughout the show that year. They devised "Red Hat," as clever a routine as you've seen on ice, in which the entire cast passes around an elusive hat that comes to symbolize, well, the pursuit of everything. And nothing at all.

"They wanted to participate in the development of the show and create a lot of their own numbers," Swain said. "They bring a lot of class, creativity, and experience and are involved heavily with Sandra in the development of the show.

"They also bring a whole other audience, a different kind of following, which adds another level of depth to the show."

The makeup of that following has changed, even if the devotion to T&D clearly has not.

"When we first started our shows in the UK in 1985," Christopher said, "we had that whole generation that already knew us. But when

"THE RED HAT" *(top and bottom)*

JAYNE TORVILL & CHRISTOPHER DEAN, "THE RED HAT"

we go back there now, children who were eight and nine years old are coming to watch the show. They weren't alive when we did 'Bolero.' It's not just the blue-rinse set, as we call them, anymore."

The standing ovations showed that the audiences—young and old—were still high on Torvill and Dean.

And on Katarina Witt. Her flowing interpretation of Madonna's "Don't Cry for Me, Argentina," was equally well received.

Katarina had gotten a reputation in some circles as a prima donna, but she fit right in with this group.

"I would say there were no failures in any of the people who joined us," said producer Byron Allen. "The perfect example is Katarina, this reputed prima donna

They [T & D] devised "Red Hat," as clever a routine as you've seen on ice, in which the entire cast passes around an elusive hat that comes to symbolize, well, the pursuit of everything. And nothing at all.

KATARINA WITT, "SCHINDLER'S LIST"

coming into this tight-knit group, this family. Kat became part of the group in very little time.

"Scott asked her to participate in his 'return to the ice' show in '97; she became that important to him."

So good was the fit that when the tour went to Germany in April 1997 and again in '98, Katarina took on Scott's role as the hostess and headliner. The '97-'98 tour also would mark the return of Brian Orser. He continued to do the Canadian tour, but had left the U.S. portion in '94.

"The first six years of my pro career, I did the whole thing with Stars," said Orser, the 1984 Olympic silver medalist behind Scott and the '88 runner-up to Boitano. "After the Olympics in 1994, they brought Kurt in. Paul was still in the show and Scott, and IMG wanted someone from that recent Olympics. I guess I was the low man on the totem pole.

"It was great to be back with Rosalynn and Scott . . . buddies from the class of '84."

"There was a little bit of bitterness, but I understood what was going on. They were looking out for the growth of the tour. That's life."

Orser's life included television specials and commentary, appearances in the Nutcracker on Ice tour, some club shows. And, of course, the Canadian Stars on Ice stops.

Still, he was delighted when IMG asked him back.

"It was great to be back with Rosalynn and Scott, my buddies from the class of '84. But I was always part of it—even when I was not there."

When skaters leave the show, they are awarded a Tiffany star, something of a badge of honor for Stars on Ice. Brian had received one in '94. He knew he had returned to the family when he had to give it back.

"At the first rehearsal when I returned, we started with a group meeting," he recalled. "They welcomed me back and everyone applauded. Then Byron—kind of joking, I think—told me to give my star back.

"I had it with me, in the bag right next to me. So I reached in and handed it back. That drew a big chuckle."

BRIAN ORSER

KURT, PAUL, & SCOTT, "FIVE MINUTES FOR ICING"

"Figure skating is wholesome family entertainment," said Smucker's Communications Manager, Vickie Limbach. "It is truly one sport that families across the country enjoy watching together."

Another big plus for the 1996–97 season was the arrival of Smucker's as a presenting sponsor. As one of its promotions, the company ran a national consumer contest called "Smucker's Sends You to the Stars," for which the grand prize was a one-week trip for four to the Stars on Ice show in New York or Orlando, with spending money, and a chance to meet the stars.

Smucker's, a sponsor of Disney World since it opened in 1971, also has been involved with the Cleveland Indians and Cavaliers, the World Series of Golf tournament, and sponsored the LPGA's Child Development Center, the first-ever traveling child-care center in the world of professional sports.

"Figure skating is wholesome family entertainment," said Smucker's Communications Manage, Vickie Limbach. "It is truly one sport that families across the country enjoy watching together. As a company with a strong family heritage, we felt this opportunity was a natural fit."

1996–97 STARS ON ICE CAST, "GUITAR CONCERTO"

Yes, and a natural part of the evolution of Stars on Ice. For more than a decade, Stars on Ice has grown steadily—as a show, as a tour, as a group. At the heart of its constant growth has been, naturally, the talent.

"Our stars keep the tour from getting stale," Allen said. "They keep it fresh. And these are such nice people. Scott brings people together.

"We've had some amazing things happen to us—wonderful, incredible things and terrible things, from Rob McCall dying of AIDS while we all watched it happen, to Sergei dying in front of all of us in our home, Lake Placid, to Scott going to Cleveland in the middle of the night from Peoria to find out about his cancer. As a result, the ties we have are incredible."

For more than a decade, Stars on Ice has grown steadily—as a show, as a tour, as a group. At the heart of constant growth has been, naturally, the talent.

CHAPTER FOUR

BEHIND THE SCENES

"We are reinventing the wheel every year. . . .It truly is like a theater presentation, and it has been a unique concept, unique to Stars on Ice."

Marvin Dolgay—music director

"When people come to see Stars on Ice, they want to see great skating, be entertained, laugh, have fun, and enjoy a total theatrical experience," Scott Hamilton said. "They want variety in the music and the production numbers and the skating. I don't think many of them care about what goes into putting on that show. That's our job."

It's not an easy job. After a dozen years of touring with the show, it actually gets more difficult, because the public has come to expect so much more from Stars on Ice every season.

This tour did not become the premier skating show on the planet by accident. It got there with diligence, determination, foresight, and good fortune.

And, oh yes, that ever-present family touch.

Off the ice, Sandra Bezic is the matriarch. It is a role upon which she insists, and it is a role in which she thrives.

"I think we work as a company, but exist as a family," Bezic said. "I am still the mom."

Michael Seibert is sort of the big brother. Lea Ann Miller is the big sister. And because both have performed in the show and also been successful as competitors,

RENÉE ROCA & GORSHA SUR

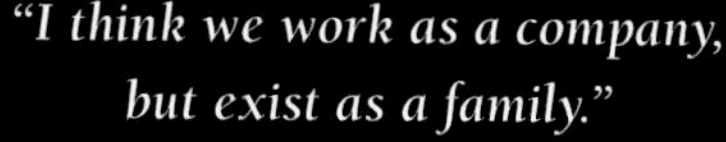

"I think we work as a company,
but exist as a family."

"The reason we work on this show for months before we get into rehearsals is that we are dealing with 12 or so stars and you must sell your ideas to them. If they are not behind what you want to do, it simply will not work. You must have them really understand and like the idea and help the rest of the cast to follow along."

MICHAEL SEIBERT, SANDRA BEZIC, & LEA ANN MILLER

they have the respect of the cast.

"I really admire what Michael and Lea Ann have done," Kristi Yamaguchi said. "They have gone from one side of skating, being out there on the ice, to the other. They remember what it was like to be in front of the crowds, performing for big audiences that expect so much."

Marvin Dolgay, the music director, and Ken Billington, the lighting designer, are the cousins with the special talents who make everything come together. Their theatrical backgrounds have been critical to the burgeoning success of Stars on Ice.

Together, this corps of creative people—several skaters call them geniuses—conceives ideas, formulate plans, and carries them to fruition. They do it every year; this is not a touring company of "Cats" or "A Chorus Line," where the dialogue and music and props and lighting don't change.

No, this is like birthing. Every year.

"Whenever I make any of these shows, my first mission is whatever is best for the skater," Bezic said. "Why? Because that is best for the show. It's my job to find that through-line and pool together all the best ideas and the most talented people to set the course."

That is one of the main reasons Bezic has insisted from the time she was hired that the production values be unparalleled and virtually unlimited. She understood that the days of shoestring budgets and scrambling around for props and costumes were memorable, but they had to be relegated to the past. Everything had to be first class for Stars on Ice, and it has been.

"You've got to spend ten times as much for lighting and music, and you've got to hire this person and that person, and you've got to trust me," she once told Bob Kain and Gary Swain, the executive producers.

"And they did. It's been fantastic. They are not a production house, and they had to learn a whole bunch of things. Now, they are respected as producers. They are not just "suits."

"It has also been my job to give my people the freedom and the proper working place to do the best they can, to bring to the table what they are capable of. IMG did that for me, and I knew if I had some challenges, I always had their backing."

DAVID HOFFIS, PRODUCTION MANAGER, WITH SCOTT

"The variety of skating and the combination of talent is what makes the production so strong. . . ."

Swain says that disagreements on production have been so rare and so minimal in scope that, well, he can't remember any.

"The variety of skating and the combination of talent is what makes the production so strong," he said. "It really is quite impressive. Look at how long we rehearse and the product we put out there on the ice, and look at the money for the costumes and the props and the production and the lights and the music and the ensemble numbers. When people see Stars on Ice, they know they will see a great show and great entertainment."

"Sandra is a master—year after year, showcasing the talents individually and collectively. She and her group have created a standard that no one else has."

The foundation of each year's show is set long before actual rehearsals begin. It's not easy to find the time for extensive rehearsing, but the planning of Stars on Ice for 1999 began before the 1998 tour was in full swing—and continued right up until the cast met in Simsbury, Connecticut, for rehearsals. It's been like that for the last half-dozen seasons.

As Seibert explained, "The reason we work on the show for months before we get into rehearsals is that we are dealing with 12 or so stars and you must sell your ideas to them. If they are not behind what you want to do, it simply will not work.

The foundation of each year's show is set long before actual rehearsals begin . . . the planning of Stars on Ice for 1999 began before the 1998 tour was in full swing—and continued right up until the cast met in Simsbury, Connecticut, for rehearsals. It's been like that for the last half-dozen seasons.

"THE RED HAT"

"One of the things that is so exciting about Stars on Ice is that the production team and creative group realize the value of the costumes— It is a key part of the show."

Jef Billings, Costume Designer.

You must have them really understand and like the idea and help the rest of the cast to follow along."

Every year, it seems, one or two of the solo numbers or ensemble routines meets with some resistance. The choreographers have come to expect that. And with so many other things going on in the skaters' lives—competitions, television specials, personal appearances, family obligations—the cast members don't always have the kind of time they'd like for working things out.

In some productions, that might make for constant tension between those on stage and those who handle the planning stage. With Stars on Ice, the tense moments are rare, though hardly unthinkable.

Just last year, there were some uneasy moments with a three-person routine

KRISTI, KURT, & KATIA, "FEVER"

involving Kurt Browning, Katia Gordeeva, and Kristi.

As Bezic explained, "If I believe in something, I will push. I think the Elvis number was a really good example. Kurt, Kristi, and Katia did not trust that they could pull it off. We showed them the choreography in Simsbury on the ice, and they sort of were looking at each other as if to say, 'Is this good?'

"But we—myself and Michael and Lea Ann—saw the potential. So I said, 'We really believe in this, trust us on this one.' They ended up loving it, and I was really proud of pushing each of them to a place where they didn't want to go. Can you get any better than those three on the ice doing something sensual?

"For Kurt, it is tough to play it straight—especially with Elvis material. He wanted to fool with it as a kind of protection. It was not a comfort zone for him,

Jef continued, "Stars on Ice is the Rolls Royce of skating shows—the total package—great skating, choreography, music and costumes, of course."

SANDRA BEZIC WITH KURT *(top)* & SCOTT *(bottom)*

but you've got to be scared sometimes. So I stand there and say to them, 'Let's just try it.' Just like a mom."

Kurt was the obedient son in that instance, and he mentioned to Bezic during the 1997–98 tour how glad he was that she pushed him to another level.

"Sandra and Michael and Lea Ann have to take the same palette and make it look different the next year," Kurt said, "with only 10 or 15 percent of the cast changing, if that much. So they are constantly trying to pull more out of each skater. As a result, I have learned so much more about my talent over the four years working with them."

Kurt believes the preseason rehearsals are crucial to the continued rising success and popularity of Stars on Ice. He went through one session of rehearsals that were too hectic, didn't have the right feel, and he found it affected the show.

"One year we went in to Lake Placid with only 10 days to light and set the whole show. Things just did not fall together. Sandra had only two or three days with the whole cast there. I felt a lot of stress among us. That is why we moved rehearsals to September. It's like a training camp." By the start of training camp, Bezic and her staff have formulated a game plan for the year.

"Skaters come to Sandra with what they want to skate to, and those ideas become her building blocks—if she thinks the ideas work," Kurt said. "Sometimes they get used, most times they don't. What Sandra focuses on is, what are we best at? How do we make ourselves look the best?

"That's the magic Sandra and everyone else off the ice performs."

Everyone—not only Bezic's group, but the individual choreographers who have worked with the performers through the years.

Sarah Kawahara and Scott have partnered on his personal numbers longer than Stars on Ice's existence. Bezic and Karen Kresge, the show's director in the first six seasons, were smart enough to recognize how well Scott and his own choreographer

"Sometimes," Scott said, "I think Sarah knows what I can do better than I do."

fashioned his routines, so Kawahara always has been encouraged to work with Scott.

"Sometimes," Scott said, "I think Sarah knows what I can do better than I do."

For Kawahara, the association with Scott has been "beyond anything I could have dreamed of in my career." The chance to work in the company of so many great skaters simply added to the reward.

"A lot of times, performers at that level have worked so hard for so long and it has been so intense that they get to a point where they say, 'I can relax now and be a show skater.' They let the technical caliber of their skating go.

"But I always believed that what makes a skater great is being able to keep what has made them as good as they are and still expand their facets as an entertainer, exploring new avenues. That is what I challenge them to do. That is the challenge all of them get in Stars on Ice.

"Scott was always intrigued by that challenge. One of the reasons he stuck with me so long, I think, is that we never wanted this year's work to be a repeat of last year's work. We are building a body of work. Stars is a perfect avenue for that."

Driving them down that avenue since 1992 have been Bezic and her cohorts. The first step is their rather intense production meetings, in which a blueprint for the coming season is hashed out. Rarely are the skaters involved at this early juncture.

"We used to have an annual production meeting with the skaters," said

SCOTT, "I LOVE ME"

(left to right) MICHAEL SEIBERT, JAYNE TORVILL, LEA ANN MILLER, CHRISTOPHER DEAN, & SANDRA BEZIC

" . . . I'll communicate with each skater on the phone, along with Michael and Lea Ann. And our production team has meetings, many meetings, where we throw ideas around."

Bezic. "Now we can't get them all in for one day. So I'll communicate with each skater on the phone, along with Michael and Lea Ann. And our production team has meetings, many meetings, where we throw ideas around.

"With the exception of Chris [Dean] and Jayne [Torvill], the skaters kind of defer to us now. Since Chris and Jayne came aboard, we have welcomed their input and they have been eager to give it."

The group sits down to analyze each skater's career and where he or she needs to go next. These choices are not made by accident, but by a careful process that evaluates each performer's progress throughout his or her Stars on Ice tenure. Or, for newcomers to the show, the production team reviews perhaps the skater's entire career before drawing up a program for the coming season.

"For example, the choices for Kurt over the last three or four years were carefully calculated to further his career," Bezic said. "And also to develop his talent. Kurt can do anything, so we want to take him down all those different roads. He will always learn from it.

"Or take Elena Bechke and Denis Petrov last year doing Led Zeppelin. It was quite a departure for them, so we said, 'We will protect you and you will look great. This might not be your main type of number, but let's give it a shot.'

"It's scary to go somewhere you haven't been, but we think it's the most important thing."

Bezic and Seibert have worked together for a decade. She hired him as her assistant for "Carmen on Ice," which starred Katarina Witt. From there, they did the Boitano-Witt tour together.

"He and I have a completely comfortable working relationship," Bezic said. "We fill each other's gaps and complement each other perfectly." Dolgay, the music director, also has worked with Bezic for 10 years. He is based in Toronto, which is convenient for Bezic, who lives in the area. She might spend several weeks in Dolgay's studio as they collect the music and he puts it together, mixing and cutting and creating.

"His understanding of figure skating and his knowledge of all sorts of different areas of music are invaluable," she said.

Dolgay had not seen many ice shows before he began his association with Bezic. He had scored a few on television, but a live tour?

"The biggest adjustment for us as a production team was we had these two units that had to merge and feel comfortable with each other and know what each other is capable of," he said, recalling the 1992–93 season. "You had the Stars family of skaters and then you had the creative team for Boitano-Witt. It was a question of us trusting their creativity and them trusting ours.

"But the melding together came pretty quick. I know from my point of view, I was comfortable with the situation almost immediately. We kept getting hired, so I guess we were doing something to somebody's liking."

Dolgay knew from the outset this would be something entirely different for him. He couldn't be sure how much leeway he would get, but he made it clear to Bezic—who made it clear to everyone else—that he was in charge of the music. Totally.

"I don't know of many ice shows that give the music director an actual job description, let alone the freedom to create," he said. "The challenge has been to define the job—within what an ice show is—and trying to bring more than music selections. It's producing an audio track with a through-line to it, with no audible edits, so it sounds like it all is composed as one piece, one seamless two-hour show.

The group sits down to analyze each skater's career and where he or she needs to go next. . . . "Take Elena Bechke and Denis Petrov last year doing Led Zeppelin. It was quite a departure for them. . . ."

KRISTI YAMAGUCHI, PETER CARRUTHERS, & DOUG LADRET IN THE "QUEEN" ROUTINE

BECHKE & PETROV, "LED ZEPPELIN"

"We are reinventing the wheel every year," he added with a chuckle. "It truly is like a theater presentation, and it has been a unique concept, unique to Stars on Ice."

One reason Stars on Ice has developed so superbly in the music area is because each side has taught the other. The performers have what Dolgay calls "skaters' ears." What they hear goes not only through their minds, but also to their feet, and they immediately think of ways of skating to the music.

Dolgay, meanwhile, is listening with his brain, imagining how it will sound for the audience. It is a strange dichotomy, but it works —especially because Dolgay knows his place.

"They are the artists," he said. "It is essential they feel comfortable."

Comfort is much more difficult in the ensemble pieces. So is formulating the music. The production people might purchase a hundred CDs and listen to them for a week to develop an idea.

MARVIN DOLGAY, MUSIC DIRECTOR

"I will take an idea from anywhere," Bezic said. "Even if it is just a germ of an idea.

"A couple of years ago, we said something about doing 'Stomp.' So we thought, 'Why not mike our blades?' Scott comes in to a meeting and says one word, like 'Stones,' and off he goes. Then we went off to research the Rolling Stones, and we came up with a wonderful routine.

"We wanted some percussion for an opening, so we pulled a classical piece in tribute to John Bonham, the drummer for Led Zeppelin, which led to the Led Zeppelin theme from last year."

Sounds simple enough, right? Hardly.

The "Fun and Games" number from 1997–98 involved 17 minutes of music, audience cheers, narration by Scott, and sound effects. Another example was in the music to a Queen ensemble routine where there were countless edits even though what the audience heard was seamless.

The other key member of Bezic's team is lighting designer Ken Billington. He also worked with her on the Boitano-Witt tour, where Bezic was awed by his work.

"We had so much more to say together," she admitted. "He brings to the table a really sophisticated and tasteful style, yet also the spectacular quality needed for a skating show for a big arena. And he enjoys the stage of an arena.

The look that has become associated with Stars on Ice is, in many ways, Billington's creation. For other ice shows and exhibitions, there might be a flurry of colors and designs at the outset of a routine or in between numbers, and, otherwise, the lighting is, well, just lighting.

"You have to consider who the skater is; what does he or she want to communicate; what is happening in their lives. A skater might say 'I was sad last year, I want to go out and be happy this year.' Or they might want to stick with what they have been doing and take it deeper".

KRISTI YAMAGUCHI, "WISHING ON A STAR"

He creates moods. . . . "But it is not a concrete thing. . . . You only can enjoy and appreciate it as you are watching it."

Billington does something else. He creates moods. He creates safe conditions for the performers. He helps the program move from one number to the next. And he does it without much fanfare.

"A lot of it is unsung, no matter where you do it," he said. "I have designed 70 Broadway shows where people come out and say, 'It's so beautiful,' without realizing it's all done with lighting. Look at 'Chicago.' Look at 'Our Town.'

"But it is not a concrete thing. There's no wood or nails or paint. You only can enjoy and appreciate it as you are watching it."

Billington usually knows the music before he gets to work. He will have listened to it and talked to the skaters. In the early production meetings, he, Bezic, and the rest of the crew will discuss the flow of the show and where each routine will fall. The crucial point here is to achieve balance—especially emotional balance.

"I always try to see where they are going emotionally with the number, then figure out how to light it," he said.

Just like the music, the lighting must work right off. Subtle adjustments can be made; otherwise, the original conception usually remains intact.

The lighting scheme is in place well before the opening show. Billington some-

TUFFY HOUGH, "QUEEN FINALE"

Billington usually knows the music before he gets to work. "I always try to see where they are going emotionally with the number, then figure out how to light it. . . ."

times will have the skaters sit in the stands and watch a run-through, complete with music and lighting. Then he'll tell them to go put on their skates and "see if they can do it."

In terms of basic technical requirements, Billington obviously must provide enough light for the skaters to perform. When skaters are doing a triple jump or a double axel or certain lifts or throws, they have to see the ice or they don't know where to land. With anywhere from 6 to 12 spotlights in their eyes, they can get confused.

When Kurt would attempt his triple axel in the 1997–98 "Fun and Games" routine—and in particular on the night he nailed the quad, 10 years after he became the first man to do one in competition—did anybody think about or recognize the importance of Billington's lighting? Kurt certainly did.

"My character, Cyril Lutz, gets to skate in white light at that point," Kurt explained. "There is no way I could try either of those jumps without it. But the lighting also just happens to be just perfect for that point in the performance."

Billington lets out a satisfied, perhaps even grateful laugh when told of Browning's praise.

"Even the greatest skaters—even people like Kurt—when they are doing terribly difficult jumps, you do have to make the lights bright. But you do it in a way within the show that the audience doesn't realize we are doing it. You work it in with music."

"My character, Cyril Lutz, gets to skate in white light at that point," Kurt explained. "There is no way I could try either of those jumps without it. But the lighting also just happens to be just perfect for that point in the performance."

Perhaps the biggest challenge for Billington is adjusting everything he does to the preferences and quirks and styles of each skater. It helps that the cast of Stars on Ice works closely with him through the lighting development, which can be tedious for the performers.

"There's no common denominator, no one special thing that works for all of them," Billington noted. "Scott might get all 10 follow spots on him. But there is not a set rule; it's whatever works for a number.

"Paul Wylie's numbers usually have dramatic music and a theme. So his lighting has to be as strong as the skating and the music he has picked. Paul understands that and will stand on the ice three or four hours while we are lighting a number.

"We'll talk about it, I create it, and then we'll run through the number as many times as we need to, and we get it clean. Paul never gets grumpy—even if it takes three or four hours or half a day. He knows it's for him and for the show.

SCOTT HAMILTON, "CUBAN PETE"

"There's no common denominator, no one special thing that works for all of them," Billington noted. "Scott might get all 10 follow spots on him. But there is not a set rule; it's whatever works for a number."

KRISTI YAMAGUCHI, "(YOU MAKE ME FEEL LIKE) A NATURAL WOMAN"

PAUL WYLIE, "SCHINDLER'S LIST"

"Paul Wylie's numbers usually have dramatic music and a theme. So his lighting has to be as strong as the skating and the music he has picked."

"After all, I'm not trying to make him stay on the ice and get cold."

Billington's assignment isn't nearly over once the lighting for a particular season is established. As Stars on Ice hits the road in the States, he has to start thinking about the Canadian tour. And about the next season, too.

"To come up with a show this size not once, but 1 1/2 times—the half is when we go to Canada—is a challenge," he said. "To keep it fresh and interesting and new every year . . . yes, it is daunting. But I'm always amazed at how well it goes."

Sometimes, the skaters think the production people can do anything. And on the other side of the coin, the production team has enormous faith in the skaters. It is this mutual confidence and respect that has made the relationship between Bezic's crew and the skaters so incredibly smooth. As Scott said, "They make us look good and we try to make them look good. We're all part of the team."

If the life of a professional skater seems hectic—particularly nowadays with

so much demand for the elite of the ice sport—consider what it's been like for the publicist who must get them here, there and everywhere.

Lynn Plage had been with Stars on Ice since before it was Stars on Ice. She began with the Scott Hamilton America Tour, providing homes for rehearsals, plus food and transportation, and has been along for every step of the slippery climb to the top.

Plage had become well-known among the small contingent of media members who regularly covered the sport. At major competitions, she ran the press facilities with such efficiency and resourcefulness—she would run back to skaters' hotels with interview requests or lists of questions to ask, then come right back to the arena with the answers—that many reporters suggested to the U.S. Figure Skating Association that it hire her permanently.

But by the late 1980s, Plage was chin-deep in handling Stars on Ice.

"When this tour first started, we would do anything we could to make it work," she said. "If it meant we had to be up at 5 a.m. to catch a flight to do 15 to 20 interviews, we did it. It was pretty hectic.

"Roz was the one who was always up to doing the media spots. And, of course, Scott, because he was the one people tended to ask for first, the gold medalist from the U.S. Kitty and Peter would always be available, too. But in the early days we had to work hard to get the interviews. The media were putting all the ice shows in the same boat; they would even get the name wrong, call us Ice Capades. Or something worse.

"We would have to say, 'We don't have MICE ON ICE!'"

Of course, once fans came to the show, they loved it and would return. But in new cities, or in the ones where attendance wasn't that great, Plage had to be aggressive—which meant hours on the phone just trying to get local newspapers and television and radio stations to commit to interviewing a cast member or two.

ROSALYNN SUMNERS, "STEPPIN' OUT"

KEN BILLINGTON, LIGHTING DESIGNER

"These people are the very best at what they do. There isn't anything in any of their lives other than being role models and heroes. When I first started pitching the show, because of that image, some people were not interested. . . . Now, America is looking for those kinds of role models. And we have the best."

These were Olympic medalists and national champions, the aristocracy of the ice. And poor Plage had to go begging for attention.

"It started getting better after 1988, when Katarina and Debi had the 'Battle of the Carmens,' and then the 'Battle of the Brians' was so dramatic at Calgary. Then ESPN and USA and Turner and the networks discovered us."

And the media discovered just how good an interview Scott and Rosalynn and just about everyone else could be.

"All of a sudden people started calling us for interviews," Plage noted. "The audiences began to realize that there were not a lot of props, that we depended on the skaters to put the show across—all these great skaters. They'd see Katia and Sergei with other pairs, or Kristi skating a solo that was magical.

"It turned out that this was what the audience wanted, not the flying people and the animals."

Oddly, in the early years, the positive vibes that emanated from Stars on Ice weren't all that attractive to the media. But, Plage said, it always came back to one thing:

(*left to right*) PAUL, PAULA ZAHN & HER DAUGHTER, KRISTI, & SCOTT TAPING "CBS THIS MORNING"

"These people are the very best at what they do. There isn't anything in any of their lives other than being role models and heroes. When I first started pitching the show, because of that image, some people were not interested. Isn't that awful!

"Now, America is looking for those kinds of role models. And we have the best."

As for dealing with the media's demands, most of the skaters find it a simple, even enjoyable experience. Others have had to learn how to handle the publicity end of the business.

"Nobody is more of a natural than Scott, and Paul has been like the intellect. Both are marvelous at it," Plage said. "I hadn't worked with Christopher and Jayne that much, but I soon learned that they really know how to promote and publicize the show.

"Kurt was not really well known in the U.S., so we pushed him to do a lot of interviews to get him better known. He's a natural. And he's so wonderful with the children at Make-A-Wish, with his great sense of humor."

Perhaps the best example of that humor—and Kurt's mischievousness—came in Chicago in 1997. A publicity day was held at City Hall, where the skaters were being presented keys to the city by Mayor Daley. A rink was set up on Daley Square on a freezing day.

Just before the skaters went on the ice, Kurt ran over to the mayor, took off his hat—nobody touches Mayor Daley's hat—and put it on his head as he skated to "My Kind of Town."

"The whole place went crazy," Plage said, and the episode made every television news show in Chicago that night.

Another media day in Chicago, when Kristi and Paul skated in the minus-20 degree temperatures on an outdoor rink to publicize the show, even made the national news shows.

Perhaps the biggest challenge for Plage was when the show truly went international, with pairs like Gordeeva and Grinkov, Bechke and Petrov, and Natalia Annenko and Genrikh Sretenski coming aboard.

"The first interviews Sergei and Katia did were in '91, from my living room, for the Stars TV show," Plage said. "They were nervous—this wasn't something they

As for dealing with the media's demands, most of the skaters find it a simple, even enjoyable experience. Others have had to learn how to handle the publicity end of the business.

GORDEEVA & GRINKOV, "THE MAN I LOVE"

were asked to do very often back in Russia—so we needed a comfortable setting.

"Katia could speak some English—he couldn't—so she did all the talking for Sergei. But he understood a lot more than he let on; sometimes Sergei would answer the questions in Russian and Katia would relay the answer in English. He was kind of a perfectionist and didn't want to speak incorrectly.

"But there were very few interviews for them while they were with the tour for those first two years. Then they went off to the Olympics in Lillehammer, won another gold medal, and everyone was interested in them. But Katia still did all the talking."

After traveling the length and width of the United States with the tour, Plage has cut back in recent years. Ironically, she chose to do so just when Stars on Ice was getting its own jet.

In early 1997, Kain suggested to tour director David Baden that they look into hiring a private jet. Baden was made the point man in finding the right airplane, which then would be customized to the tour's needs. After a three-month search, Baden and Byron Allen, Stars on Ice's producer, found what they were looking for in Oklahoma City.

"It was by no means cheaper than commercial flights or buses," Baden said, "but every year we have enhanced the tour on the production end, and now we wanted to enhance the quality of life for the skaters."

Although most of the Stars on Ice family has fond memories of the long bus rides, the overnighters, there weren't any complaints about this new step up in transportation.

"It really was a luxury for some of us who had been with the tour for a long time," Allen said.

"All of these people are stars who want to do their best. If someone mails it in, they all know it. Everybody in the building knows it. So if there is anything we can do to assure their success, their comfort, we try to do it."

Quality of life to match the quality of skating. Makes sense.

"The schedule had gotten so tough and so demanding, we felt getting our own plane would lessen the burden, and it did. It keeps the skaters healthier; it enables

(clockwise from top) THE '96-'97 STARS ON ICE TOUR BUS; NOVOTNY & KOVARIKOVA, SCOTT, LARA LADRET, DAVID BADEN, ROSALYNN, & KAREN PLAGE ON CHARTERED FLIGHT; SCOTT & ROSALYNN ON THE 96-'97 STARS ON ICE TOUR BUS; ROSALYNN ON THE STARS ON ICE PRIVATE JET

DINNER AT DIMILLO'S IN PORTLAND, MAINE—A CAST AND CREW CLOSING NIGHT TRADITION

us to stay longer in the cities when we want to and get out of cities we want to leave. We don't have to wake up early, deal with limited commercial flights—even commuter flights—then rush to do the show.

"Instead, the flight crew is ready after each show, and there's full catering. It's a festive atmosphere, and everybody can relax."

Everybody means the skaters, three members of IMG—usually Allen, Baden, and Deb Nast, the talent-media coordinator and one of the chief liaisons between the cast and tour managers—performance director Doug Ladret and one of two physical therapists, Martina Schmelova or Lara Ladret. There is a strict policy not to fill up the plane with other people, so that it remains a private place for the skaters.

The new arrangement brought back some special travel memories, good and bad.

There was the night in 1994 Rosalynn came closest to missing a show—in Philadelphia, no less, with fiancé Bob Kain's family and friends attending at the Spectrum.

"I was used to putting my skates on top of the bus heater to let them dry off," Roz recalled. "Well, I left them on the bus."

Not normally a problem, except the bus had already left for the next tour stop—in Florida. Baden and company called local skating clubs looking for the right kind of skates, and wound up having to drive to Wilmington, Delaware, about 30 minutes from Philadelphia, in order to find the right kind.

"They weren't broken in, so I could skate in the show but couldn't do the jumps," Rosalynn recalled with a shudder, followed by a giggle. "Close call."

There are also the airport stories, like the time Kristi, Scott, and Isabelle Brasseur—an Olympic medalist who with partner Lloyd Eisler skates on the Canadian tour—were eating "big, sloppy burgers" at a restaurant. A woman came up to them and asked for autographs.

Kristi and Isabelle, fine ladies that they are, wiped their hands and signed. The woman then turned to Scott, who had just taken a huge bite out of his burger.

"He looked up and gave her a big smile, with the food still in his mouth, and reached for the pen," Isabelle said. "She realized, very embarrassed, that this was not the best moment for an autograph."

"He looked up and gave her a big smile, with the food still in his mouth, and reached for the pen," Isabelle said. "She realized, very embarrassed, that this was not the best moment for an autograph."

Baden and Paul had quite an adventure getting to Lake Placid for rehearsals one October. They left Boston around ten o' clock at night for a drive of perhaps four hours. But Paul got stopped for speeding in upstate New York. The officer, not a skating fan, did not recognize the name Paul Wylie, and not only gave him a summons, but prohibited him from driving the rest of the way.

"Paul had a stick shift and I don't drive a stick," Baden recalled. But not wanting to disobey the officer or chance more serious sanctions by getting stopped again, Paul slid over to the passenger's seat and Baden got behind the wheel.

"We drove the rest of the way to Lake Placid with Paul working the gears and me trying to work the clutch. We got there at about 5 a.m., with rehearsals that morning."

Not that travel difficulties completely disappeared with the hiring of the private jet. With the tour in full swing during the heart of the winter, weather is a major consideration every night.

"Our second flight was from Charlotte to Greensboro," Baden said. "You wouldn't expect to hit bad weather at the end of December in the Carolinas, but we hit a snowstorm. When we get out to the runway to start de-icing the plane, well, they are not used to doing that in Charlotte. They quickly ran out of de-icing fluid, so they got out there on the wings with push brooms and were pushing the ice and snow off.

Not that travel difficulties completely disappeared with the hiring of the private jet. With the tour in full swing during the heart of the winter, weather is a major consideration every night.

"Everyone was bug-eyed: Should we be getting off this plane?"

The flight went smoothly, but it was the last plane allowed into Greensboro that night.

"But without our own plane, we might not make that show," Baden said. There are some stops the tour would never want to miss.

At the top of Scott's list is New York, particularly Madison Square Garden, which he has called "the mecca."

"There's such a vibrant feeling there," he said. "It always gets your juices flowing. It's always one of the most exciting nights on the tour. New York has to be the best show."

It doesn't hurt a bit that, in recent years, the Garden party has been a sellout.

Another favorite, a recent addition to the tour, is the Arrowhead Pond in Anaheim, California, where the tour also draws well. Several skaters called it "the prettiest arena we play."

THE CAST & FLIGHT CREW INSIDE THE PRIVATE JET

TORVILL & DEAN, "TAKE FIVE"

"From the makeshift dressing rooms, they had to go outside, walk through mud surrounding the building, and take an elevator up to the ice. I remember Christopher Dean was running late, so there he is, part of the greatest ice dancing couple in history, standing in the Texas air, waiting for an elevator to get him up to the rink surface."

"The thing that amazes me—knock on wood—is in my years on this tour we've had such incredible experiences," Baden said, "but this tour runs so smoothly that there are very few war stories." And so many nice ones.

There are other, less majestic places that have become a part of Stars on Ice lore and remain dear to the hearts of tour members. Hersheypark Arena, the home of the Hershey Bears minor league hockey team in Hershey, Pennsylvania, is hardly a shining showplace. But it is a special stop for the cast.

"It has an intimacy that's hard to match anywhere," Paul said.

Added Baden: "In the new ones, the acoustics are so good that the crowd noise is absorbed and the skaters don't sense the crowd as much. But in the older buildings the fans are right on top of the skaters, and it enhances their performance."

Baden doesn't have such kind words for all the older arenas, however. The 1996–97 stop in Austin, Texas, for example.

"It was an old shed, a barn, with no dressing rooms and no showers," he said. "They put pipe and drapes up to make dressing rooms. It was sort of nostalgic for the skaters, I guess. You know, 'This is how it used to be a long time ago.'

"From the makeshift dressing rooms, they had to go outside, walk through mud surrounding the building, and take an elevator up to the ice. I remember Christopher Dean was running late, so there he is, part of the greatest ice dancing couple in history, standing in the Texas air, waiting for an elevator to get him up to the rink surface.

"But then we look out the entrance door and see this line of cars coming up this zigzag road. I thought I was in the middle of 'Field of Dreams.' You know: If you build it, they will come. And the fans loved the show."

There have been similar scenes in comparable buildings across America.

"The thing that amazes me—knock on wood—is in my years on this tour we've had such incredible experiences," Baden said, "but this tour runs so smoothly that there are very few war stories." And so many nice ones.

"I did a lot of the bus trips," Plage recalled, "sleepovers in bunk beds, leaving at night from the hotel to get to the next city. I was always in the bottom bunk, and on one of these trips I remember wondering, 'What am I doing sleeping on a bunk on a bus going from one city to the next? What kind of a job is this?'

"Then Roz leans over her bunk and says, 'Goodnight, I love you.'

"And I thought, 'That's why I am here.'"

KRISTI YAMAGUCHI, "MADAME BUTTERFLY"

CHAPTER FIVE

THE TRAGEDIES

"It is going through things together that bonds you. You get stuck on the road and have to walk 25 miles with someone, then you've got something there to share."

Kurt Browning

One of the most striking things about Stars on Ice is the togetherness, the camaraderie, the fellowship. Unlike professional sports teams, where players tend to go their own way during and after the season, this troupe is a tight-knit group.

It is more than friendship. It is kinship—ties that bind in special ways. Kurt Browning has been with the tour full time only since 1994, yet his observations apply to a dozen years of devotion that have marked Stars on Ice.

"It's seeing people mature, watching Kristi, for example, from when she was a teenager training in Edmonton and seeing how much of a grown-up and well-rounded woman she has become," he said. "We all have changed as we've grown older together. But we all love each other and love to skate.

"One thing seems to be at work: We can bitch and make fun of each other; I can complain about members of Stars on Ice, but you can't.

"It is going through things together that bonds you. You get stuck on the road and have to walk 25 miles with someone, then you've got something there to share.

"Also, not many people in the world get to create something with each other,

It is more than friendship. It is kinship

—ties that bind in special ways.

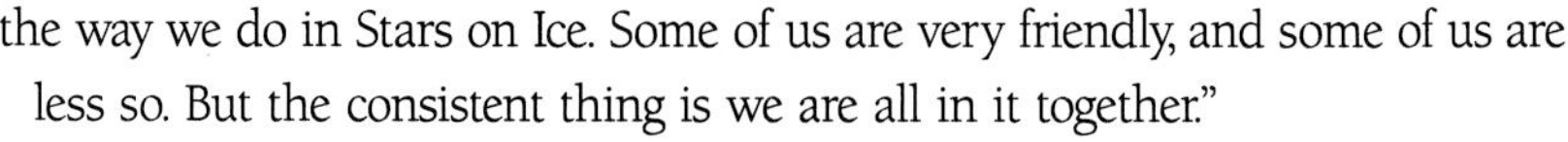

the way we do in Stars on Ice. Some of us are very friendly, and some of us are less so. But the consistent thing is we are all in it together."

That togetherness has been tested during the most tragic times—with the deaths of Rob McCall and Sergei Grinkov.

Rob and Tracy Wilson won a bronze medal at the Calgary Olympics in ice dancing, before a home crowd "that lifted us right up there onto the medals stand," Rob said at the time. When they opted to turn pro, it was clear where they should go: to Stars on Ice. "We wanted to add to what we had done as skaters and take it one step further," Tracy said. "The chance to do ensemble work really appealed to us. So did having creative input with a small group of star skaters. "We were really motivated coming out of the Olympics and not ready to pack it in. We were ready to try something different."

"Rob and Tracy had an incredible sense of humor and wonderful rapport with each other and everyone else."

Very different. No longer would they have weeks to train for specific dances at periodic competitions. Instead, they had to get their routines down in perhaps a week of rehearsing, then perform them night after night. They also had to quickly master their portions of ensemble numbers.

"At first," Tracy said, "it was quite terrifying. But then everyone made us feel so at home right away.

"It could be quite chaotic. There were no safety nets, and you had to rely on each other to kind of get through it. We had to talk each other through the group numbers, find out who knew the steps and who to follow."

Tracy and Rob had trained with Brian Orser for years, so the three of them joined the tour for the 1988–89 season almost as an entity. And they quickly became fixtures on the ice and behind the scenes.

"Rob was one of the people who brought humor into the show," Scott said. "Rob and Tracy had an incredible sense of humor and wonderful rapport with each other and everyone else.

"Rob was always making people laugh. He'd be trying to do triple jumps in

practice to show everyone that an ice dancer could do them."

Rob also was the tour's "King of Cards"—so dubbed by Scott and Brian and Billy Fauver.

"He brought to the tour a card game called 'Kaiser,'" Scott recalled. "It was an actual game, but only Rob knew all the rules, so we would kid him about having invented it.

"The teams were always the same: Brian and Billy against Rob and me. We'd have these full travel days with no show to worry about, and Rob would mix up a batch of Bloody Caesars for everybody. Once he got a few in him, he would be brilliant, and it was almost as if we were psychic. We could not be beaten after a few of those drinks."

More often, however, they would lose to Brian and Billy, and Rob and Scott would accuse their opponents of concocting secret hand signals to tell each other how to bid.

In addition to his "King of Cards" moniker, Rob was also the king of

. . .they quickly became fixtures on the ice and behind the scenes. "Rob was always making people laugh. He'd be trying to do triple jumps in practice to show everyone that an ice dancer could do them."

"They were going to be as good as anybody ever," Scott said. "They had great contact with the audience and great vision."

tardiness—he held the record for fines for being late for the tour bus—as well as the king of room service.

One night, Lynn Plage and Brian arrived in Detroit after a media day in Providence. When they reached the hotel and headed to their rooms, they saw a waiter with a loaded room service cart heading down the hall. They followed it, with Plage betting Brian that the meal was headed for Rob's room.

This was at about 10 p.m. on an off day, meaning the skaters had had plenty of time to tour the city's finer restaurants. But sure enough, the waiter went to Rob's room. When he opened the door, the meal was delivered by the publicist and the skater.

At least Rob ate his own food that night. He was notorious for eating off of other people's plates.

"At least Tracy would ask, 'Are you going to finish that?'" Scott said. "Rob just reached over and took food off your plate."

Rob also was a practical joker. When he first met Tracy, she was a 16-year-old volunteer at Skate Canada in Vancouver. One day Rob pointed to a young couple near the ice and told Tracy they were French-Canadian and spoke no English. He asked her to help them find their way.

So the ever-helpful Tracy wandered over and began giving the couple instructions in the simplest English imaginable. Of course, the pair turned out to be American.

"He loved nothing more than to tell a story at your expense," Tracy said. "He just had a different way of looking at things, totally unconventional."

By the end of the 1989–90 tour, Tracy and Rob had reached new levels in their skating.

"They were going to be as good as anybody ever," Scott said. "They had great contact with the audience and great vision."

But Rob began feeling weak toward the end of that season. In Richmond, he was having trouble catching his breath and was coughing a lot. He and Tracy were scheduled to join the Boitano-Witt tour after Stars on Ice concluded its season, but Rob didn't make the rehearsals for that tour.

"Nobody was aware of how sick he was, and it seemed strange he missed a show," Tracy said. "He appeared healthy, but just had some trouble breathing. A number of skaters around the industry had gotten sick at that time of year. It seemed to be a really bad cold."

It was much worse. It was AIDS.

"It seemed so quick," Bob Kain recalled. "Even in those days, nobody knew much about being HIV positive." Plage, who sent him homemade chocolate chip cookies when he was hospitalized—he would share them with the nurses—also visited Rob at his home just before he died.

"At that time he was looking very good and very upbeat," she said. "I had lunch with him and felt he was doing very well. He had no hair, and I told him he looked like a young Yul Brenner."

Rob McCall died on November 19, 1991.

"It was a huge kick in the gut for Stars on Ice," Billy said. "He was a huge personality. That was one of the things that signaled the end of the first generation of Stars on Ice."

Tracy has became a fixture on both Canadian and American television as a skating commentator. But her career on ice came to a halt when Rob became ill.

"We all loved him," she said. "Rob was very honest and very bright and very funny."

"It was a huge kick in the gut for Stars on Ice," Billy said. "He was a huge personality. That was one of the things that signaled the end of the first generation of Stars on Ice."

The romance only developed after Katia and Sergei had become champions.

Gordeeva and Grinkov. G&G. Katia and Sergei.

No pairs team in skating history has stirred the passions of the masses the way this one did. She, the wisp of a teenage skater, seeming to float along the ice—or in the air when he lifted her, carried her, threw her. He, the foundation of the team, the rock on which its masterful routines were built.

By the 1988 Olympics, they already were world champions. At Calgary, they became the world's pair, an impossibly young yet inconceivably brilliant duo. In a sport where it was supposed to take years, even a decade, to reach the gold medal level, they had done it in almost no time at all.

"When they skated, you didn't hear any noise," Scott said. "They moved along the ice with such speed and grace and almost in silence. Even when Sergei would lift Katia, there was almost no noise and seemingly no strain. You remember things like that because you almost never see them in skating.

"And they were so made for each other, on the ice and off."

The romance only developed after Katia and Sergei had become champions. Their on-ice performances always hinted at it, but there was a four-year age difference: she was 11 when coaches teamed her with the then-15 Sergei.

Katia always stood by Sergei, right from the beginning. A coach once complained that Sergei missed too many practices and insisted Katia leave for another partner. Instead, Katia left with Sergei for another coach.

The loyalty was reciprocal. When Katia hurt her foot and was placed in a cast, she fretted that Sergei would look for another partner. Instead, he supported her. On New Year's Eve of 1987, with perhaps a bit too much vodka in his blood, Sergei kissed her for the first time.

They joined Stars on Ice in 1991 and stayed for two years. That second season was Kristi Yamaguchi's first with the tour.

"When I first joined the tour, the first year or so I was still in awe of Katia and Sergei," Kristi said. "I think I watched them every night. I loved their skating—my all-time favorite pair."

When the eligibility rules changed in 1993, Katia and Sergei were among the professionals who went back into training for the Lillehammer Olympics. They had enjoyed their golden moment at Calgary, but they also felt a need to go back.

"We left to become professional skaters when we were so young, and we felt that maybe there was more to achieve," Katia said before the Lillehammer Games. "We didn't want to have that question in our minds.

"We were very excited when the rules were changed. We believed we could show the people what we had learned from being on tour in Stars on Ice. We are better skaters now, a better pair. We have learned to be more artistic, and we have been very careful to be technical, too."

"When they skated, you didn't hear any noise. . . ."

Katia was right, so right. The defending champions, Natalia Mishkutienok and Artur Dmitriev, were majestic, powerful, and precise—many thought their performance was worthy of gold. But G&G were almost heavenly in their free skate, to "Moonlight Sonata." Their return to the Olympics was enchanting.

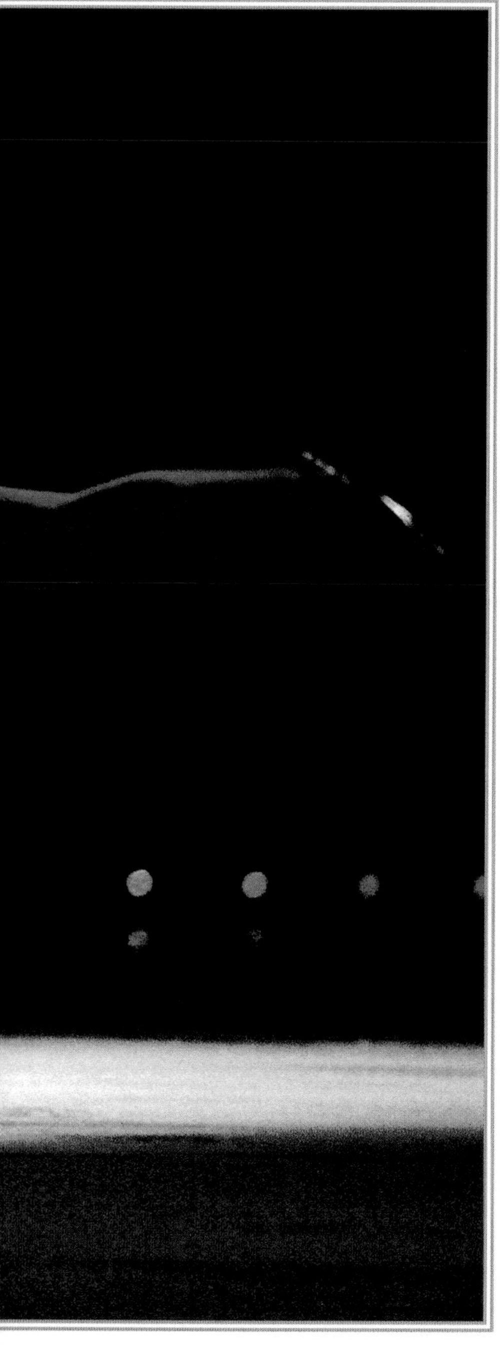

"I believe we made a very wise decision," Katia said after the gold medal performance. "This is a great moment for Sergei and myself."

The question for them now became, What next? The first answer was a family; Katia had given birth to Daria in 1992. The second was, happily, a return to Stars on Ice.

"We expected and hoped they would come back to the tour," Bob Kain said. "At that time everyone thought they were the best pairs team in the world, maybe of all time.

"Our plan was to invite them back and convince them, even with a baby, that this was where they would fit best."

It helped that Russians Elena Bechke and Denis Petrov, another exquisite pair, and dancers Natalia Annenko and Genrikh Sretenski were with the tour. But there also were more Russians on the Champions on Ice tour, which featured many skaters with remaining eligibility.

The decision was easy, Katia said. Stars on Ice had become, well, like family. "We had made so many friends and we felt so close to the people in Stars on Ice," she said.

And when they did return, according to Kain, "They really were better than ever. After Lillehammer, they started to become not only great quality skaters, but started to work as ticket sellers, more than any pair team of our time. And the skating world was blossoming then."

As was Stars on Ice. It was hitting all the big cities, it had added the biggest of skating headliners.

Life was almost perfect for Katia and Sergei.

"We expected and hoped they would come back to the tour," Bob Kain said. "At that time everyone thought they were the best pairs team in the world, maybe of all time. Our plan was to invite them back and convince them, even with a baby, that this was where they would fit best."

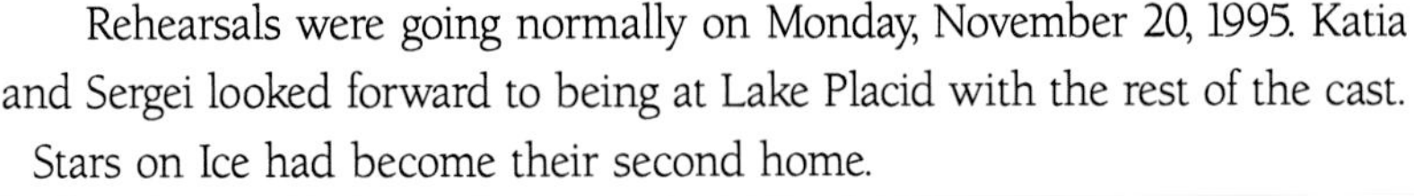

Rehearsals were going normally on Monday, November 20, 1995. Katia and Sergei looked forward to being at Lake Placid with the rest of the cast. Stars on Ice had become their second home.

In the middle of their practice, they stopped skating.

"Everything seemed to be fine," said Laura Nardiello, a skate instructor and one of a handful of people present when Sergei collapsed. "They went into their routine a little bit. He lifted her, put her down, and then just stepped back.

"Gordeeva asked, 'Are you OK?' He said, 'I just feel a little dizzy.'"

Katia helped her husband sit on the ice. It would be their last moment together in this life.

Sergei lay down and lost consciousness.

He was defibrillated three times on the ice by rescue workers, twice more in the parking lot, then rushed to Adirondack Medical Center in nearby Saranac Lake. Sergei Grinkov never regained consciousness. He was 28 when he died.

"He was like a pillar. . . .He was strong and silent, and just very, very caring."

"I was in Cleveland when I got the call from Roz saying Sergei had gone unconscious on the ice and looked blue and that they were all scared to death," Kain recalled. "She said medics were there within a minute or two.

"We had phone lines into the hospital and into the Lake Placid building, and I was getting updates constantly. It must have been within an hour that they told me he was not regaining consciousness. I think I knew he was dead then."

When Kain received official word, he had to tell the skaters. They had gathered together at the hotel, praying, crying, holding each other. Some were hysterical. Making that phone call "was an unbelievably hard thing to do," he said.

The troupe had been through tragedy before, but nothing could compare to this. Rob McCall's death was painful, but he also was far removed from Stars on Ice when it occurred.

"Sergei was right there one minute, gone the next," Paul Wylie said. "There is no way to describe the pain and shock of that."

"He was like a pillar," Kurt added. "He was strong and silent, and just very, very caring."

Kain chartered a plane and flew to Lake Placid, where the entire Stars on Ice crew was mired in confusion and denial and just plain shock.

"Byron and I worked with the Stars on Ice staff and skaters while Deb Nast and Jay Ogden (Katia's managers) went to work for Katia." So much had to be done, including alerting family members, and making funeral arrangements in the United States and Russia. But one thing had to take precedence: Katia herself.

Sandra Bezic and Michael Seibert got all the skaters together, while Katia was back at her house.

"They weren't sure if they should go over to see Katia," Kain recalled, "and I said, 'Go, be with her and hug her. If she doesn't want you to be there, she can go into a bedroom. Go hug her and show her we love her.'"

The cast members and crew drove to see Katia in virtual silence, save for the sobbing. How would they greet her? What could they say? How was she holding up under the worst of circumstances, the cruelest of horrors?

"I can't ever remember a more difficult and emotional time," Kristi said. "But Katia was unbelievable, she was so strong. I will always admire her strength."

The group didn't stay for long. It wasn't necessary.

"I knew they loved me," Katia said. "I knew they would always be there for me."

Soon after, Kain held another series of meetings on what to do about the tour, which was due to open in Lake Placid in a few days. They decided to continue to rehearse and stay together, but to postpone the show.

During the next few days, it was determined that Sergei died of too big a heart. While anyone who knew of his kindness and love for his family and devotion to his friends could have testified as to the size of his heart, it was, in reality, a medical condition that killed him.

An autopsy showed Sergei died of a massive heart attack caused by a blocked artery in an enlarged heart plagued by high blood pressure.

"He was clearly in very good health except for this one problem," said Dr. Francis Varga, who performed the autopsy. "Athletes' hearts are frequently enlarged, but his heart was disproportionately enlarged."

Sergei was buried in Moscow on the same day Stars on Ice was to debut for the season in Lake Placid. The cast had continued rehearsing. . . .When they returned, their heavy hearts told them the right thing to do. . . . Ten days after Sergei's death, the 1995–96 tour debuted at the Olympic Center in Lake Placid.

"Unless his condition was discovered and he had a bypass, it was only a matter of time. Many times in young people the first sign of coronary artery disease is sudden death."

Those findings caused a stir in Russia, where Dr. Lev Markov, of the Moscow Sports Health Center, said it was a misdiagnosis.

"We have had several such cases when an athlete's heart starts growing," Markov said. "It can become as much as twice the normal size. It causes a variety of heart dysfunctions and can cause such a sudden death."

However, a special medical test can detect the disease, according to Markov, and Sergei showed no signs of the problem.

"In 1994, when we examined Grinkov for the final time before the Olympics, we didn't find anything wrong," Markov said. "I doubt the diagnosis of the American doctors saying that he died from a heart attack."

Nevertheless, the autopsy confirmed the diagnosis.

Sergei's death was front-page news in many Russian newspapers. G&G were true Russian heroes, and both his passing and his funeral were treated as if he had been a head of state.

"It is hard to believe that Sergei is dead. . . . He was not only a great sportsman, he was an open, easy person. It was always a pleasure to talk to him," said Valentin Piseev, chairman of the Russian Skating Federation.

Memorial services were held throughout Russia and at several Russian Orthodox churches in the United States.

Scott and Paul journeyed to Moscow for the funeral, along with Jay Ogden and Deb Nast, who had become Katia and Sergei's confidant on the tour, and who remains one of Katia's closest friends and advisers.

"The loss of Sergei will never be thoroughly understood or accepted," Scott said. "But having shared in his perfection is something we can carry with us always.

"Kurt said the only flaw in their Olympic program was that it wasn't long enough. I guess that applies to Sergei's life as well. We only had him for a short while, but he lived a life of incredible quality. Knowing that makes his passing only slightly easier to take."

Sergei was buried in Moscow on the same day Stars on Ice was to debut for the season in Lake Placid. The cast had continued rehearsing, then everyone left upstate New York for Thanksgiving weekend. When they returned, their heavy hearts told them the right thing to do.

"We had to put on a great show for Sergei and Katia," Scott said.

Ten days after Sergei's death, the 1995–96 tour debuted at the Olympic Center in Lake Placid.

"We couldn't get it all done fast enough, and I hope you understand," Scott

told the crowd. "What we're presenting, on Sergei's shoulders, is the best we've got, and I'm sure it's going to be good enough. We're going to give you something real special."

The show's first act closed with a tearful introduction by Scott of "G&G," inviting the spectators to close their eyes and imagine the pair was on the ice. Grieg's "Concerto in A Minor," the music to which Katia and Sergei would have skated, echoed through the arena.

Kristi said it was the most difficult performance she had ever skated. Rosalynn agreed, as did Paul, Kurt—heck, the entire cast.

"I don't know why this happened, but I know that in a special way Sergei has touched my life," Kristi said. "The warmth of his heart and the love he gave to his family, to skating, and to life is what resulted in his perfection on the ice. Not only was he part of the greatest pair team ever to skate, he was an even greater man."

After the heart-wrenching show, with barely a dry eye in the house, Elena Bechke put it best.

"This romance will last forever," she said, wiping tears from her eyes, "because they love each other as nobody else can."

The show's first act closed with a tearful introduction by Scott of "G&G," inviting the spectators to close their eyes and imagine the pair was on the ice. Grieg's "Concerto in A Minor," the music to which Katia and Sergei would have skated, echoed through the arena.

Katia searched for a way to honor her husband. Each time she looked at Daria, she saw Sergei, too. And she saw a need to be part of something, a tribute above all others for her lost love.

"The idea of turning the Hartford show into a special tribute to Sergei seemed to make the most sense," Kain said. It was scheduled for the end of February, so the crew would have time to develop something truly wonderful.

Katia had the chance to go back to Russia for awhile in the meantime.

"We went to CBS to see if they would do a prime time special," said Kain, "and we would invite some close friends of Katia and Sergei into the show. Then we would take all the money raised from the evening and start a fund for Daria.

"We kept everybody busy thinking about how to do it, and we got Sandra and Michael and Lea Ann to start working on it. I think that was better than sitting around shell-shocked."

What nobody knew was that Katia planned to not only preside over the tribute, but skate in it.

Together with choreographer and close friend Marina Zoueva, Katia put together a routine. She had not skated with anyone but Sergei since they were first paired by Soviet sports officials in Moscow in 1982. But she would perform—alone—in "A Celebration of a Life." She would skate solo to Mahler's Fifth Symphony.

What nobody knew was that Katia planned to not only preside over the tribute, but skate in it. . . . "This is going to be my first step, and I hope people will appreciate it."

"This is very different and a very important day for me," Katia said. "I cannot compare it with the Olympics or any of the competitions, because they always have been with Sergei. This is going to be my first step, and I hope people will appreciate it.

"It was very difficult when we created this number. The first two to three days, it was hard to do anything. The old feelings were very fresh and my thoughts were very sensitive."

Each time she took the ice to practice, she felt the unfillable void of Sergei's absence. At the same time, she was filled with desire to make everyone understand what Sergei had meant to her. And what skating means to her.

"I skate for Sergei and hope the people will remember him each time I take the ice," she said. "I know that we could skate together beautifully and I know that we had a lot of fun, and I know that we had confidence, and I know when we were going to skate well. But now I am one, and I don't know if anyone wants to watch me and I don't know how I am going to skate by myself."

Ah, but everyone wanted to watch her, and they would be transfixed by her presence that night in the Hartford Civic Center.

"I will never again skate on the same level as I skated with Sergei," she said. "It was the highest anyone can think of skating. But it was another life, and now is another life in which it is more important for me just to find the strength to skate and to be a mother.

"I really want this night to be a celebration of life. Sergei really loved life and he always tried to inspire me with the same feeling—that life is not only about skating, but is beautiful itself."

"I really want this night to be a celebration of life. Sergei really loved life and he always tried to inspire me with the same feeling—that life is not only about skating, but is beautiful itself."

"A Celebration of a Life" would feature many of Sergei's favorite numbers. In addition to the Stars on Ice cast, performers included Viktor Petrenko, who had known Sergei since he was 12, Oksana Baiul, ice dancers Marina Klimova and Sergei Ponomarenko, Brian Boitano, Yuka Sato, Alexander Fadeev, and 13-year-old Fedor

The mood before the performance was not jovial, but it was not somber, either. . . .Paul picked "Apollo 13," the uplifting soundtrack to the film about man's ability to respond to even the greatest challenge. At one point, he blew a kiss heavenward. . . .There were also lighthearted numbers, because, as Scott said, "Sergei loved to laugh. I could always make him laugh." So Scott did "Hair"—Sergei's favorite of all the Hamilton routines. . . .

Andreev, the son of Zoueva, who had become Katia's constant companion since Grinkov's death.

The mood before the performance was not jovial, but it was not somber, either.

"We each want to have a role in remembering Sergei," Paul said just before the show. "We each want to contribute a special moment as a memory to him.

"I think seeing Katia yesterday [at the practice rink] eased all of us. We were a little nervous about it, and very excited about her wanting to skate."

But there were doubts about how well she was handling it.

"Just watching Katia throughout the day, it seemed like it would be really difficult for her to perform," said Scott. "She seemed to be getting a little pale during rehearsal and we were all very concerned for her.

"But when it came time to do what she wanted to do and pay tribute to Sergei, the courage and strength and determination and love really came shining through."

The program began with piano music from Beethoven's "Moonlight Sonata," and the crowd was absolutely silent as 19 skaters dressed in black and white took the ice.

They formed a circle—a circle of champions, featuring three Olympic men's winners, two Olympic women's gold medalists, pairs and dance champs, the very best skating has to offer. Then, one by one, they left the circle, moving to other places on the ice.

Scott, Kristi, Paul, Kurt, Rosalynn, Elena and Denis, Katarina. All of the guest stars.

Suddenly, all eyes were drawn to the scoreboard, as a video of G&G's 1994 Olympic performance was presented. On the ice, Oksana and Kristi were crying. In the audience, nearly everyone else was, too.

Then came the solos.

Elena and Denis, so often competitors of G&G in another time, at another level, did their signature routine about two lovers who could not be together, set to the music of "Spartacus."

The elegant Klimova and Ponomarenko also did their most famous program, to Tchaikovsky's "Romeo and Juliet," a story of love unfulfilled, of permanent, painful separation.

Paul picked "Apollo 13," the uplifting soundtrack to the film about man's ability to respond to even the greatest challenge. At one point, he blew a kiss heavenward.

Oksana, dressed in black and skating to "Ave Maria," finished on her knees and hands, praying. And sobbing.

There also were lighthearted numbers, because, as Scott said, "Sergei loved to laugh. I could always make him laugh."

So Scott did "Hair"—Sergei's favorite of all the Hamilton routines—and Kurt went with "Brick House," a number he said "always gave Sergei a charge."

Fadeev, a world champion just when G&G were getting started, skated to a medley of Elvis tunes. Sergei loved Elvis, too.

Then there were the more direct tributes, such as Viktor's "Have You Ever Really Loved a Woman?" by Bryan Adams. And Rosalynn's "Remember Me This Way," sung live by Jordan Hill.

It was all so touching, so heartfelt, so supportive.

Yet it all seemed incidental once Katia took the ice.

"We had to put on a great show for Sergei and Katia," Scott said. Ten days after Sergei's death, the 1995–96 Stars on Ice tour debuted at the Olympic Center in Lake Placid.

She stopped, covering her face, understanding that he was gone. She searched the ice for him, circling, wondering where he was, why he was gone. . . .She dropped to her knees, leaned over and kissed the ice. The mind's eye saw her kissing his grave, saying goodbye—forever.

The packed arena seemed to hold its collective breath—skaters, fans, family, and friends—as a single spotlight lit the blue ice. The crowd rose as one, the applause built and lasted a half-minute, even as Katia skated to Mahler's Fifth Symphony.

Wearing a white and bluish-gray dress, Katia moved slowly as she held out her hand, as if skating with a partner. But no, Sergei was not there.

She stopped, covering her face, understanding that he was gone. She searched the ice for him, circling, wondering where he was, why he was gone.

She dropped to her knees, leaned over and kissed the ice. The mind's eye saw her kissing his grave, saying goodbye—forever.

She looked skyward as if to once more ask why. One final time. Then she fortified herself, skating around the rink with grace and power and self-assurance. She spun. She jumped. Yes, she even smiled.

This was the girl Sergei partnered. This was the woman Sergei loved. This was her tribute to him.

Mahler's piece ended. Katia, her eyes awash in tears, skated to where her daughter sat and took three-year-old Daria in her arms. Then she put her daughter down and hugged Ana Grinkov, Sergei's mother. Finally she hugged Zoueva warmly. And she was gone as the house lights came on to signal the end of the first act.

For the finale, the entire cast—all in white—took the ice and paired off. Then Katia reappeared, wearing a traditional Russian costume with headpiece. Skating through the couples—who were posed in positions that started G&G's different routines through the years—she joined with Scott.

But for only a brief moment. Katia then skated, jumped, and spun around the ice to Tchaikovsky's Symphony No. 5. Alone, for sure. Yet ready to take on the challenges ahead.

Alone, for sure. Yet ready to take on the challenges ahead.

Scott brought Daria to Katia again and told her, "For as long as you need all of us, we'll be here for you."

"I don't have enough words," Katia said to the audience at the end of the two-and-a-half-hour show. "But I also want to wish to every one of you: try to find happiness and at least once a day, smile to each other. Every day, say just once, I love you.

"It is so difficult to talk. I want you to know I skated today not alone. I skated with Sergei. That is why I skated so good."

As the crowd stood once more, cheering warmly, lovingly, the skaters took turns embracing her. Scott brought Daria to Katia again and told her, "For as long as you need all of us, we'll be here for you."

After they'd left the ice and the crowd had filed out, many of the skaters remained in the caverns of the Civic Center, too drained to even pack up and leave. Or maybe they sensed a certain presence in the building, and they wanted to be near it for just a little longer.

Katia understood that she had to make the Hartford performance a beginning, not an end. She knew Sergei would want it that way.

"I have a lot of things to say to people," she said, "a lot of things to show people, and the ice helps me with it. I have a lot in my soul and I want through my skating to show it."

There would always be a place for her to show it—with Stars on Ice.

"They are people who believe in me," she said. "I didn't believe that I could skate by myself. They showed it was possible."

But Bezic insists it is Katia who has contributed something special to Stars on Ice, not the other way around.

"Katia has taught us so much," Bezic said. "The thing about Sergei and Katia is they were so elegant as people, and so undemanding and professional. They were refined.

"Without Sergei, she has blossomed in a way that maybe she would not have under his protective arm. She had to go out on her own. I can't imagine what that has been like for her, but she always carried herself with so much dignity."

As Kristi put it, "Obviously, there was the initial shock, and I know there were some difficult times, some nights on the road, when she told me she doubted whether she belonged out there, whether it was something Sergei would have wanted. Yet she still was able to get on the ice and improve and find another part of the sport that she loved.

"And it's been fun to see her come out of her shell, to see those bright eyes looking at the world, trying to observe everything. Before, she and Sergei were kind of in their own world, sheltered, but she had to step out of that.

"Katia was half of what everyone considered the perfect pair. And then to go and skate singles and when you have never done it at all, that is incredible."

Which is exactly what the last few years have been like for Katia, now an accomplished soloist, and for Stars on Ice. The two-fold challenge—to come up with routines that fit Katia, and for Katia to master those routines—has been met superbly.

Katia has been part of ensemble numbers, and she has been on her own. She has done classical and she has done Elvis. She has gone from Bach to Bonham, from George Gershwin to Led Zeppelin.

"When I saw her solo for the first time," Katarina said, "I stepped back to the boards to watch, and she was so delightful. It's so wonderful for me to see how she found her spirit and how she's doing what she's loved to do all her life.

"She's been through a tragic time with her husband's death, but you almost forget when you see her. I mean, you do forget, which is nice, because you should watch her and enjoy her skating and not think about the sadness."

Exactly. Because, thanks greatly to her place in Stars on Ice, it no longer is about the sadness.

"She is something exquisite, completely exquisite," Bezic said. "We would all like for her to be the artist she is. But do you know how hard that is, to go under the spotlights alone if you've never done it? It is so difficult."

But, as Katia has proven, it is so possible. And so necessary.

Sergei would have told her that.

✯ CHAPTER SIX

SCOTT

"Every day should be celebrated. Every day should be beautiful. You have to find a way."

Scott Hamilton

Scott Hamilton knew all about cancer, had seen the worst it had to offer. His own mother had died of the disease. So when the disease hit him in March 1997, he was prepared to battle it. And this was a battle he was going to win.

"I saw what my mother went through and how brave she was. That was a major factor in my facing it without crumbling—a great source of inspiration." Just as Scott's courage would inspire countless others.

But even before his mother's illness, Scott had become acquainted with adversity—and with overcoming hardship. Dorothy and Ernie Hamilton adopted Scott in 1959. Ernie was a college professor and Dorothy taught in an elementary school. They were a comfortable couple with a daughter, Susan. A few years later, they would adopt Stephen.

During his early childhood, the life that awaited Scott would have been difficult for the Hamiltons to imagine. Their dream was simply that Scott might have a day without pain. There was very little sunshine in Scott's early life, perhaps a reason he became such a gregarious person and enchanting performer.

Scott was in and out of hospitals for much of his first eight years. He was

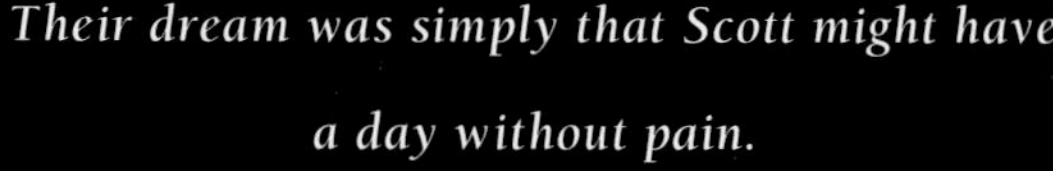

Their dream was simply that Scott might have a day without pain.

That exercise became skating. And the trauma of his early years would fade for Scott once he discovered the ice.

diagnosed with various illnesses, including cystic fibrosis and celiac disease. He was placed on a special diet barring all dairy products and such things as cookies and candy. He often was too weak to play outside at recess with the other students, remaining in the classroom doing schoolwork or playing with toys. Alone.

At one point, Scott subsisted mainly on a pink liquid he called "YUCK." Doctors put a feeding tube into his stomach that came out through his nose and was hooked up to a bottle of the stuff. It was annoying and embarrassing.

Scott persevered. His parents never told him about the doctors' diagnoses, but he understood he was not well. He never heard, as Dorothy and Ernie often did, that Scott was going to die before his tenth birthday. But he hated the isolation from other kids. He hated the pity he heard in adults' voices.

When Scott was in the third grade, a family friend and physician told the Hamiltons he believed their son did not need the special diet. To prove his point during a weekend vacation with the Hamiltons, Dr. Andrew Klepner told Scott to eat whatever he wanted. Should he become ill, Dr. Klepner said he had the necessary medicines to treat it.

Scott ate ice cream and donuts and peanut butter and . . . he never had to subject himself to YUCK again.

In 1967, again on Dr. Klepner's advice, the Hamiltons took Scott to Boston Children's Hopsital, where cystic fibrosis and the other diseases were ruled out. Doctors determined Scott had a partially paralyzed intestine. The correct diet and plenty of exercise would take care of the problem of his stunted growth.

BLACKHAWKS HOCKEY TEAM—1969, SCOTT *(first row, far left)*

That exercise became skating. And the trauma of his early years would fade for Scott once he discovered the ice.

But tragedy would not leave his life. In 1974, Dorothy was diagnosed with breast cancer. For the next three years, it would hold her in its death grip.

"My mother was a very strong woman, very determined," Scott says. "She tried not to let anything beat her, and she tried to keep me from seeing how much she was suffering. She wanted me to be successful as a skater and was afraid of holding me back because of her illness.

"When I found out about my cancer, I did say pretty strongly to myself, 'I can get through it again.' I was never concerned whether I would be able to get by it; I was positive I could get through the whole thing.

"But one thing I feared was the pain. I didn't mind the chemo and feeling sick, but I worried about the pain I saw my mother go through. It was devastating."

The Stars on Ice tour was in East Lansing, Michigan, when Scott began "feeling crummy." He'd experienced pain in his abdomen and believed he might have an ulcer. Or maybe it was his 39-year-old body telling him to slow down, that so many nights in so many towns doing so many shows was just too much.

During rehearsals for the East Lansing show, Scott hurt his back. He could barely stand up straight and certainly couldn't get through his jumps. After a quick examination by a physical therapist, Scott was told to see a specialist.

Naturally, the showman made sure the show went on that night. But he was in severe pain afterward as the tour headed to Peoria, Illinois.

"Scott's pretty good at keeping a happy face," said Kurt Browning. "He hid this one pretty well, too. We really didn't have a clue how bad he was feeling."

On the morning of March 16, Scott went through a battery of tests at the St. Francis Medical Center in Peoria. He didn't expect the verdict: a cancerous tumor in his abdomen. And it needed to be removed quickly.

"He called me at home early on Sunday evening," Bob Kain recalled. "He said, 'Bob, I have a problem, this big tumor. I think it is cancer.'

"'But I want to skate the show tonight. I think I can do it.'

"I said, 'Are you kidding?'"

Scott returned to the arena, where all of the skaters had noticed his absence from rehearsal.

"We hadn't heard any complaints from Scott," said Rosalynn Sumners. "But he was not at the warmup and everyone was wondering, 'Where is he?'

"Somebody told us he was having some hospital tests, routine stuff. But when he came back to the arena, Scott was limping and pale and it looked like something big, some real trouble.

"I called Bob, but Bob said he'd already talked to Scott and that we should do the show, then Scott would have something to tell us. That's when I knew it was serious. I watched Scott's face all night. But the son of a gun, he never let it show."

Indeed, Scott called that evening's performance one of the best of the year.

"It was a special night. To get through that finale and not be able to say good-bye was very hard . . . a really challenging show. Just getting through that show probably helped me get through the next four and a half months.

ERNIE HAMILTON, SCOTT'S FATHER

"My mother was a very strong woman, very determined," Scott says. "She tried not to let anything beat her, and she tried to keep me from seeing how much she was suffering. She wanted me to be successful as a skater. . . ."

"I remember what a friend of mine, a comic named Mack Dryden, who also had cancer, had told me. He said that when you tell somebody about having cancer, you give it to them, too. What he meant was that everybody else isn't sure how to handle it, just as you aren't sure. It can become very uncomfortable for everybody."

Trying to handle the situation as comfortably as possible, Scott personally told each of the cast members just what was going on. He called Karen Plage, his girlfriend, and asked her not to worry, but Karen said she was flying to Cleveland and would meet him at the Cleveland Clinic Foundation, considered among the top cancer hospitals in the United States. Scott would take more tests and treatment there.

During that season, for the first time, Scott had given himself a present, a rock star's type of tour bus, which he used for many of the non-airplane trips. Kain told Scott to get in the bus, drive up to Cleveland, and park it next to the Marriott Hotel. The next morning, Kain picked him up and they went to the clinic together.

Scott underwent tests nearly all day. When doctors didn't detect any swelling in the testicles, they thought he might have lymphoma, which does not have nearly the cure rate as testicular cancer.

He called Karen Plage, his girlfriend, and asked her not to worry, but Karen said she was flying to Cleveland and would meet him at the Cleveland Clinic Foundation. . . .

"The waiting was so hard, not knowing what it was, or what kind it was," Karen Plage said. "Scott was sure, but I kept being optimistic."

Added Kain: "After they analyzed all the tests and the biopsies, it was about midday on his second day in Cleveland and we were in this doctor's office—Karen, Scott, and myself. Then six white coats come walking in, single file. They said, 'We know what it is, exactly. It's testicular and it is crystal clear. The tumor is growing very quickly.'

"So Scott goes, 'Oh, whew, I thought it was something serious.' The doctors all look at him, then go on and on about how serious it is. I finally said, 'He knows it's serious. He was just relieved it wasn't something else.'"

Scott was relieved that his cancer was treatable, but he was all too familiar with the gravity of the situation.

"When somebody tells you that you have something like this, it's an instant shock," Scott said. "It's especially hard when someone close to you has gone through it. But my attitude had a pretty quick turnaround. It was, 'All right, this happened, what's next? How do we fight it and beat it?'"

Beating it would not be easy, but the success rate for dealing with testicular cancer is quite high. The next day, Scott underwent more tests, CAT scans on his chest, and MRIs. Doctors found the chest and the brain were clear.

Still, the tumor was huge, twice the size of a grapefruit. It had to be shrunk

SCOTT IN A GARTH BROOKS MEDLEY

through chemotherapy, which presumably would kill the cancer. Then the tumor and Scott's right testicle, which caused the cancer, would need to be removed surgically.

Only three days after the tumor was discovered, Scott met with the cast and told all of them what was ahead. All twelve Stars on Ice stars bused from Dayton to Cleveland to have lunch with him and to lift his spirits. Scott wound up doing the cheering up.

". . . I watched Scott's face all night. But the son of a gun, he never let it show."

SCOTT, "HAIR"

"We had a real fun time," he said. "That's what makes everyone in the show so special. We're together so much, we have such camaraderie and such a feeling of family. We rally around each other and we feel the pain everyone else feels and the happiness everyone else has."

"You don't take somebody like Scott Hamilton out of a performance and not miss something."

Because the tour was virtually over—less than a month remained—Scott's absence did not have a huge effect on attendance or overall performance. It did, however, remain a source of worry and inspiration for the other skaters.

"There wasn't a day we didn't ask about Scott or find out how he was doing or what was going on," Paul Wylie said. "There were some nights where it didn't seem natural without Scott on the ice. But that made all of the skaters in the cast want to make each night special.

"There were some nights where it didn't seem natural without Scott on the ice. But that made all of the skaters in the cast want to make each night special."

"You don't take somebody like Scott Hamilton out of a performance and not miss something. I believe each of us wanted to add an element to our performance that said, 'This is for Scott and what he means to us and to Stars on Ice.'"

While Scott underwent chemotherapy in both Cleveland and at home in Denver, questions about the future of Stars on Ice surfaced for the first time—not from IMG or Scott or the other cast members, but from the media. Reporters and commentators asked whether Stars on Ice could continue to flourish without its originator.

With Wylie not planning to remain much longer—a career in business or law had beckoned for a half-dozen years and he would retire at the end of the 1997–98 season—would Browning be able to carry the men's side of the show? Would the producers seek new stars such as Ilia Kulik, Elvis Stojko, Philippe Candeloro, or Todd Eldredge when they likely would turn pro after the 1998 Olympics?

"We are always looking for new talent," said executive producer Gary Swain, "but we know you just don't replace a Scott Hamilton; someone has to grow into that role. Kurt is really coming on in the role of showman, but even so, Scott's personality is so unique.

"Scott is the statesman of figure skating. And he has transcended the normal skating following to bring people in who may not have had a lot of interest in skating."

Scott never wondered. He was going to come back and he would do so in style.

"My only real concern was if I could get back to the level of proficiency of before," he said. "But I also would take with me back to Stars on Ice the attitude that this is one thing that will make me a better person.

"I really wanted to consider this a very short and temporary part of my life. And I would never focus on the negatives. Basically, I laughed a lot and did whatever I could . . . to keep up the positive thoughts."

There were days when such optimism was difficult.

"He came home to Denver," Plage recalled, "and he was tired a lot, and it's hard to see him like that. There were a few days with a lot of energy and we'd go to the movies or out to dinner or he would play golf. But some days, Scott just did not have his usual energy, and those were the toughest days."

One thought in particular kept Scott focused on his recovery: How would it feel to get back on the ice?

"I know for the last 29 years, being a skater and seeing people in the audience and being able to entertain them has meant a great deal to me," he said. "It has given me pride and pleasure, and I am not ready to give that up.

"I want to retire on my terms. When I no longer enjoy it, I will stop. I was really enjoying it last year, having a great year. I love my job and that is inspiration enough."

Inspiration enough to fight through the days of nausea and chills and weakness from the chemo treatments and injections of Bleomycin, a cancer-fighting drug.

"I met Brett Butler of the Dodgers when he was in Colorado playing the Rockies. We sort of compared notes, me on my form of cancer, Brett on his throat cancer. I spent ten minutes with him and I know nothing is going to slow him down. In a way that helped me a great deal.

"We can send out a message that cancer is something you can beat; it is treatable and you can fight it. What's important is just the awareness that it can happen to anyone. Not to make anybody paranoid, but it is not a bad idea to go in and get checked. No one has to go through what I did. If you catch it early enough, it is a blip."

"Scott is the statesman of figure skating. And he has transcended the normal skating following to bring people in who may not have had a lot of interest in skating."

The six months of treatment and recovery were not total hell. Scott spent more quality time than ever at home with Karen. She even convinced him to shave his head when clumps of hair began falling out from the chemo.

Still, being away from the ice for the longest stretch in more than three decades was hard for Scott Hamilton.

In June, his AFP marker in his blood was tested. A normal reading is below ten, but Scott's had been 8,800 when the cancer was discovered. By his last chemotherapy, it was back to normal.

The surgery late in June removed the tumor, now the size of a golf ball, and the right testicle also was removed.

"The only time I thought he was scared was the night before surgery," Kain said. "He knew if they pulled out all this dead stuff, it was all OK. But if they found anything active, it would be a whole new path of chemo. There were a lot of anxious moments. He was frightened.

"But the surgery went great the next day and there was nothing left in there. That was like the last chapter, and thank God."

He lost weight during a weeklong stay in the hospital, when he could not eat solid foods. His muscle tone was gone. His stamina? Forget it.

So Scott's anxiety built through the summer. When could he finally put the skates back on? When could he rejoin Stars on Ice and begin rehearsing?

How would his body react to getting back on a rink? Would he be able to stand up?

Jumps? Could he do a single lutz, let alone a double or a triple? Would he have to discard his trademark backflip?

"Life is an adventure," Scott said. "Every day, there's a brand new challenge. Whatever it is, it's never a cakewalk. It's not meant to be easy, and I learned it's not meant to be fair. It's what you make of it, where you take it, how you deal with it.

"Every day should be celebrated. Every day should be beautiful. You have to find a way."

Scott began finding his way back to the ice in early August, and on August 9, he "became whole again." He stepped onto the ice in Simi Valley, California, with choreographer Sarah Kawahara by his side. This was the first test.

"S-H-A-K-Y," he spelled out. "It was very shaky. But it was necessary."

SCOTT, "FIVE MINUTES FOR ICING"

Scott couldn't remember the last time he was so nervous before taking the ice. Certainly not since his Olympic-eligible days.

Other cast members were just as apprehensive.

"We all wanted Scott to come back in such a strong way that it would be like he never was off the ice," Yamaguchi said. "Of course, that was selfish on our part, but we knew that Scott would give it everything, fight as hard as he could, to get back to the level he was skating at. He just needed the time to do it, and none of us were sure how long it would take. But we knew he would try."

He has an unbelievable passion for skating and for Stars on Ice. . . .It is his legacy, I guess, what Scott has given back to the sport."

SCOTT, "STEPPIN' OUT"

Added Sumners, "With Scott, we knew it was the most important thing to him to get back on the ice, get back with the tour. He has an unbelievable passion for skating and for Stars on Ice. Nothing else in life is as important to him. It is his legacy, I guess, what Scott has given back to the sport."

With those first tentative moves on the ice in Simi Valley, Scott was making it clear he was coming back. But it didn't happen overnight.

"I was uncoordinated and very weak," he recalled. "It was not a very pleasant experience.

"Sarah was walking me through it with footwork and exercises to see what I could do. But it really was a devastating first day back, a real disaster. I couldn't do anything.

"I tried to do a spin and three turns in, I got dizzy. I wasn't even about to attempt a jump. A backflip? Not a chance."

Kawahara was somewhat unprepared for that. Scott had told her he planned his return to the ice for before they would meet in California. She expected he would have already eased his way back into skating, and that their sessions would be more fine-tuning than back-to-the-beginning work.

SARAH KAWAHARA WITH SCOTT

Scott made things even tougher by bringing along a pair of new skates. It was typical of Scott in a way. In the face of adversity he is really good.

"I knew we would be working on a different level, but I thought he would have his sea legs—his ice legs—under him," she said. "It was kind of a shock.

"I think he just wanted to do it with somebody, and I am so glad it was me. He was apprehensive, afraid of what he might feel, or not feel. It was really great, just the two of us on the ice, in privacy."

Scott made things even tougher by bringing along a pair of new skates.

"When I realized he had not broken in new skates and it was his first day back—I mean, nobody comes to me with new skates. Well, Scott figured he might as well break it in all at the same time, his body and new skates. It was typical of Scott in a way. In the face of adversity he is really good. It seems like the bigger the mountain, the stronger he pushes back. He wanted to make sure the mountain was as big as could be and so he threw the new skates on top."

The next day, not feeling sore or achy or weakened by the first test, he was back on the ice. It still wasn't going well, but at least Scott felt more comfortable.

After three days, Kawahara could see a big difference; his timing and rhythm began to resurface. Five days after his disastrous return, all of those wonderful moves that were second nature to him began coming together. He still had balance problems and he was limited to simple double jumps, but Scott felt he was progressing. As did Kawahara.

"What he said to me was the chemo really destroyed his muscle tone and he felt he really had to build that back up. It was a harsh reality to face, but Scott is such a fighter."

The process of working his way back to a level he considered worthy of the tour—just being able to do a few jumps or skate one easy number would never be enough—was difficult. Scott had periods of self-pity, even anger about what he had gone through. Most doctors say that's natural for cancer patients. It was extremely unnatural for Scott, however, and his attitude annoyed him.

"I realized I was skating like a cancer survivor instead of skating like a healthy person," he said. "I was thinking about all the massive toxins and chemicals in my body . . . the anesthesia . . . the major surgery.

"That's no way to live. Every day, I'm thankful for my health. Every day, I'm grateful there was treatment and a cure for what happened to me. At the same time, that's behind me. It's time to get back to a normal life."

While Scott slowly got back into performing shape, a show in his honor was being planned for October 29 in Los Angeles. It would be a tribute to his

SCOTT, "STEPPIN' OUT"

distinguished career—a valentine to perhaps the most popular skater ever. And it would be a reaffirmation of Scott's role in the figure skating world. Taped for television by CBS, the show included nearly the entire Stars on Ice cast, plus special guests such as Brian Boitano and Olivia Newton-John.

One of the highlights of the show featured such cohorts and friends as Yamaguchi, Boitano, Browning—just about everyone who has been associated with Scott through the years—performing renditions of his trademark routines.

"He didn't know they were going to do that," Karen Plage said. "We tried to keep a few things in the show secret, which is not an easy thing to do, but we succeeded and he loved it. All these years of work and his best friends were paying tribute to him. He couldn't ask for anything more."

"Every day, I'm thankful for my health. Every day, I'm grateful there was treatment and a cure for what happened to me. At the same time, that's behind me. It's time to get back to a normal life."

(clockwise from top) BRIAN BOITANO, "IN THE MOOD"; KURT BROWNING, "HAIR"; KRISTI YAMAGUCHI, "WHEN I'M 64"; BRIAN ORSER, "CUBAN PETE"; *(special costume designs by Jef Billings)*

While Scott sat at rinkside, he watched the entire cast spoof "Hair". Then Yamaguchi did his "When I'm 64" and Katia Gordeeva performed a spot-on version of "I Love Me". He saw Brian Orser in a wonderful departure from his usual style, playing "Cuban Pete," a character as identified with Scott as Rhett Butler was with Clark Gable and Browning finished with "Walk This Way".

The costumes for the show were designed by Jef Billings, who had been a huge part of Scott's career, and Kawahara had developed all of those numbers with Scott.

"That was an extra bonus," she said. "Our relationship has gone far beyond my wildest dreams in terms of longevity and the variety of work we have done together and collaborated on. When we did that comeback special, I really was able to sort of look at that whole passage of time and our 13 years together and the years of Stars on Ice, and it was a neat feeling—very special."

Then it was Scott's turn. More nervous than he'd been since, well, his Olympic days, he took the ice to perform to country star Gary Morris' live rendition of "With One More Look At You" from "A Star Is Born." It would become Scott's signature routine for the tour. Some would say it was his message that this would be his final year with Stars on Ice, and the 1997–98 tour would provide his legions of fans with one last view of skating's most beloved performer.

ROSALYNN SPOOFED SCOTT IN HIS "OLYMPIC TRIBUTE" ROUTINE

Although he was far from in top shape and his skating—particularly the jumps—was rusty, the sight of Scott Hamilton back on the ice was mesmerizing. The utter joy he was experiencing seemed to radiate throughout the Great Western Forum. When he was finished, when the crowd was on its feet, cheering and weeping, calling his name, asking for more, Scott felt overwhelmed.

"I WIN!" he said when handed a microphone. "I always knew I was going to get back to where I was before. Tonight was an indication that it's going to happen and I'm going to be right where I was last year."

That meant right back on tour, right in the middle of the action.

But tour organizers were wary of placing too much burden on Scott too soon. Although the tour would not begin in earnest until after Christmas, nobody was certain how much of a role Scott could play.

"When we were planning the show in July and August, he wasn't even back on the ice regularly," said Michael Seibert, the tour's associate director and choreographer. "You have to be responsible to the show and the planning, so you don't box yourself into a corner when you've got such an unknown."

. . .the show featured such cohorts and friends as Yamaguchi, Boitano, Browning—just about everyone who has been associated with Scott through the years—performing renditions of his trademark routines.

That's exactly the way everyone wanted it. Especially Scott. "I don't want the focus to be on anything but the skating," he said. "This is not about me and dealing with cancer. This is Stars on Ice, a night for everyone to just sit back and enjoy the best skating."

The 12th season of Stars on Ice once again would premier at the Olympic ice rink in Lake Placid on Thanksgiving weekend.

"Lake Placid was another very emotional show," said Kain. "The year before, we welcomed Katia back, then we had Scott coming back in this performance. Lake Placid has definitely become the home of Stars on Ice, with all the emotions that go with a family."

This tour would feature more versatility than ever. Orser returned for the entire tour. Katarina Witt was on hand for a portion of it. Ice dancers Renée Roca and Gorsha Sur had become more accustomed to the touring life and the nuances of the show.

Scott was healthy enough that he didn't need to accept a diminished role in the show. In fact, he would perform a 6-minute, 23-second solo called "The Show Must Go On."

The highlight of the program figured to be Scott's solo to "With One More Look at You." But the varied repertoire, heavy on Led Zeppelin at the outset and for the finale ("Stairway To Heaven," naturally), and including the works of Elvis Presley, Count Basie, Louis Armstrong, John Williams, Neil Diamond, and Paul Simon, created a flowing pace throughout the show.

That's exactly the way everyone wanted it. Especially Scott. "I don't want the focus to be on anything but the skating," he said. "This is not about me and dealing with cancer. This is Stars on Ice, a night for everyone to just sit back and enjoy the best skating."

Scott was healthy enough that he didn't need to accept a diminished role in the show. In fact, he would perform a 6-minute, 23-second solo called "The Show Must Go On."

At the outset of that routine, the crowd is informed that due to uncontrollable circumstances, all nine parts in a tribute to "The Wizard of Oz" will be portrayed by Scott Hamilton. He then goes from playing a Munchkin to the Scarecrow to the Tin Man to the Cowardly Lion to the Wizard himself,

1997–98 CAST, "LED ZEPPELIN"

SCOTT, "THE SHOW MUST GO ON"

The other showstopper, which closed the first act, was inspired by Torvill and Dean, the most accomplished ice dancers in skating history. Entitled "Fun & Games," and written by Ed Swift, the author of Gordeeva's book in tribute to her late husband, My Sergei, *it was one of the cleverest routines in Stars on Ice annals.*

SCOTT AS THE NARRATOR, "FUN & GAMES"

TORVILL & DEAN, "THE RED HAT"

with barely a moment to catch his breath or his bearings.

"It's a big, fun, crazy number," he said, "longer than I thought it would be and very demanding. It's for kids—adult kids and kid kids."

Providing something for everyone always has been the aim of the tour. The other showstopper, which closed the first act, was inspired by Torvill and Dean, the most accomplished ice dancers in skating history.

Entitled "Fun & Games," with dialogue written by Ed Swift, the author of Gordeeva's book in tribute to her late husband, *My Sergei*, it was one of the cleverest routines in Stars on Ice annals.

With Wylie playing the part of coach Evian Merry (the coaches who oversaw his competitive career were Evy and Mary Scotvold), and training Yamaguchi (Anne Ne'eragain) and Gordeeva (Lily Pureheart) to be Olympic champions, the routine was a hilarious send-up of the entire skating industry. It also featured Browning as rising star Cyril Lutz, a bundle of nerves when the competition begins; Roca and Sur as the tandem of Gorky and Park, who after an initial failure find a way into the hearts of the judges (yes, they do have hearts); and Sumners as the quintessential skating mom, Ivana Medal.

Torvill and Dean, Orser, and Elena Bechke and Denis Petrov were the judges, and Scott served as narrator throughout one of the most memorable ensemble numbers in the dozen years Stars on Ice has thrilled audiences.

"Who better to make fun of what we all know and love and make our livings from than all these Olympic champions?" asked Seibert. "The fans love it, and who else is there?"

Actually, the skaters loved doing it, too.

"You have to be able to laugh at yourself, goof on yourself and your surroundings," said Browning, who does a triple axel on cue during "Fun & Games," in which he gets to win an Olympic medal, something he never achieved before turning pro.

Browning was so good at his part that, on the 10th anniversary of hitting the first quadruple jump in competition—at the 1988 world championships—he did another quad.

"I was on a country music talk show in Nashville and they reminded me that it was 10 years to the day since I did the quad," he said. "I hadn't realized it. I decided to go to the rink and see if I could do one in practice.

ROSALYNN AS IVANA MEDAL, "FUN & GAMES"

1997–98 CAST, "FUN & GAMES"

"Who better to make fun of what we all know and love and make our livings from than all these Olympic champions? The fans love it, and who else is there?"

I thought, 'Wouldn't that be cool.'

"I did one and everyone kind of clapped and cheered and that was about it, but it got me thinking that maybe there was still some magic there. Cyril Lutz gets to skate in white light, because it is supposed to be at the Olympics. So there was plenty of light, and I said, 'Maybe I should just try it.' I didn't tell anyone, because if it was not feeling right, it would be a waste.

"When it was time for the triple axel, the skaters who play the judges were wondering why it was taking so long to set it up. Then I threw the quad in it and hit it quite well. Scott freaked out and I freaked out and totally dropped character. I was just so excited because it was the 10th anniversary and I landed another quad.

"Scott yelled out, 'A quad,' and the Nashville crowd went wild."

Scott remembers the season opener at Lake Placid as not the best performance of his career but one of the most important.

"There were some nerves, but I also felt very confident that what I had done over the past few months I had done in the right way," he said. "It was the only way I could be ready for the tour, and this was the time to show I was ready."

SCOTT, "WITH ONE MORE LOOK AT YOU"

"Scott has gone from a very big star to a megastar, the king of skating. He's taken the Stars on Ice tour with him."

He was ready, and he was back. Everyone knew that—everyone on the ice, everyone in the stands, everyone who has a special attachment to figure skating.

"By that time," Kain said, "Scott had moved to another level. He had a cover of *People* magazine, and all these stories in all sorts of media. His story created another profile of Stars on Ice that made it even bigger.

"Scott has gone from a very big star to a megastar, the king of skating. He's taken the Stars on Ice tour with him."

Still, Kain knew that even with the solid show on Thanksgiving weekend, Scott still had much to prove to himself. When the full tour began on the West Coast, he was struggling to hit any triple jumps, and it bothered him tremendously.

"I showed up at San Diego, and then they were going to L.A. and Anaheim.

"Scott really wanted to show people he was all the way back," Kain said. "So the son of a gun hit his triple lutzes those nights and nailed his shows perfectly. When I saw him, he gave me the thumbs up."

Scott always has loved the bright lights of Broadway. While Madison Square Garden technically is not on the Great White Way, symbolically it represents everything to an athlete that Lincoln Center does to a diva or the Shubert Theater does to a thespian.

When the tour reached New York City on March 14, Scott already had performed at the Garden more than 50 times. This, however, would be the most memorable of those Garden parties.

Five days earlier, Scott, Kristi, Katia, Kurt, and Paul spent a day in New York with children from Make-A-Wish. They held a skating clinic for them, then enjoyed a lunch together at the All-Star Cafe.

During the luncheon, several of the youngsters presented the skaters with home made ribbons and medals. One fifth grader already was taller than Scott.

"It's such fun for us to get the opportunity to spend a day like this with these kids," Scott said. "This is the one time through the year we are able to meet the kids and I can relate to them, especially now.

SCOTT WITH A CHILD FROM THE MAKE-A-WISH FOUNDATION

"We do 60 tour cities with Discover Stars on Ice, and there is a little pressure for us to stand up in front of 17,000 people. But part of why we do it is the chance to associate with Make-A-Wish and these kids."

"It's such fun for us to get the opportunity to spend a day like this with these kids," Scott said. "This is the one time through the year we are able to meet the kids and I can relate to them, especially now."

Added Kristi, who also is shorter than some of the Make-A-Wish children, "If we can inspire these kids to go after their dreams, it is so great."

Many of those kids were in the audience at a sold-out Garden for the show. They had no idea that the night's proceedings would conclude with a bonus that would almost overshadow the Stars on Ice program itself.

For months, in secret, Garden officials made plans to induct Scott into the Walk of Fame. He would be the first figure skater so honored.

The Walk of Fame is the most prestigious award any arena presents. Among the inductees in New York are the greatest athletes and entertainers—Muhammad Ali, Michael Jordan, Wayne Gretzky, the Rolling Stones, and Frank Sinatra, to name a few—ever to play the Garden.

Keeping such an honor a secret was not easy. Just ask some of the cast members.

"I was so nervous all week, thinking I might give it away," Kristi said. "You know, just one slip, like 'I can't wait until Saturday.'"

But Katia, perhaps sensing that any obvious nervousness on the part of Scott's skating family would be a giveaway that something was up, said she tried to treat the New York show like any other.

What a show it was!

"We were on right from the start," Kurt said.

But it was the finish that everyone would remember.

As "Stairway to Heaven" concluded, the cast took its bows while the crowd—including the likes of Tara Lipinski and Oksana Baiul—stood in tribute. All 13 skaters stood side-by-side at the far end of the rink, arms linked as they bowed, their usual stance for the conclusion of the show.

Then Kristi turned to grab a microphone from a Garden official and said, "Tonight, we have something different . . . a very special presentation."

Then Kristi turned to grab a microphone from a Garden official and said, "Tonight, we have something different . . . a very special presentation."

"We're sitting and watching and Kristi grabs that microphone and she never does that," Karen Plage said. "I had no idea what was going on. I could see Scott was wondering what was going on."

Kristi introduced MSG vice president Bobby Goldwater, a longtime friend of Scott's, who took the microphone near center ice. Scott still had no clue what was happening.

"There are 46 people in the Walk of Fame," Goldwater said. "We've never had an occasion in its five and a half years to induct someone from the world of figure skating. We have that occasion tonight."

The crowd, sensing where this was leading, roared, and Scott bowed his head, understanding now.

"Twenty years ago, he came here in Super Skates. More than 50 times since then, he has skated here," Goldwater continued. "He is part of Madison Square Garden history forever.

"In the world of figure skating, there is no finer representative than Scott Hamilton."

After sharing warm hugs with his fellow performers, Scott skated over to Goldwater to accept a plaque commemorating the moment. Then he turned to Kristi and Rosalynn and Kurt and Paul and the others and, with a smile, he scolded them for their subterfuge.

"There are no secrets in this company," he said with a laugh.

"I am totally at a loss."

KRISTI, "LED ZEPPELIN"

Scott Hamilton speechless? Well, just for a few seconds.

"There is no better audience in the world than a New York audience," he shouted to the hugest ovation yet. "You've been giving me goosebumps for 20 years.

"This sheet of ice has given me so many incredible moments, and this is another. To see a show I started 12 years ago be filled to the rafters is THE BEST.

"I'm extremely humbled by this. I can't believe I'm the only skater in—Dorothy [Hamill] is going to be SO MAD. And to be inducted in front of Tara Lipinski, the next generation. . . .

"It's been kind of a rough year for me and one goal is to do the entire tour, and the show that means the most is this show. You've just turned it all around and I'm going to tour next year for sure.

"New York, you've given me so much. To be part of this amazing building and its history means so much."

With that, Scott began a tour of the rink, holding the plaque high, sharing it with the folks in the front row and the fans in the balcony. Sharing it with all the other skaters on the ice—and all the others who have performed with him for a dozen years in the epitome of all ice shows.

Yes, this award was for Scott Hamilton, the most endearing of all skaters. And for Stars on Ice, the most enduring of all skating shows.

SCOTT, "HUNGARIAN RHAPSODY"

CHAPTER SEVEN

LOOKING AHEAD

"We have been carried for the past six years by Kristi and Scott and Paul and Kurt and Jayne and Chris and Ekaterina. . . .It's important to add youth to the mix. . . ."

Byron Allen—producer

The 1998–99 season brought some notable cast changes to Stars on Ice. Torvill and Dean, while still choreographing some routines, decided to stop performing. Katarina Witt, meanwhile, opted to appear only in some of the European shows.

But six new faces appeared on the roster, including both the male and female Olympic champions. As Bob Kain said so many years ago, enhancing the cast with the brightest of stars always remained the priority.

So Tara Lipinski, fresh off becoming the youngest figure skating gold medalist in Olympic history, joined the tour. And along with the perky teenager came Russian Ilia Kulik, whose victory at the Nagano Games was highlighted by the most difficult free skate ever seen.

"We have been carried for the past six years by Kristi and Scott and Paul and Kurt and Jayne and Chris and Ekaterina," Byron Allen said. "It's important to add youth to the mix, and we couldn't do better than add the two reigning gold medalists.

"Tara has been the first everything, the youngest everything. She won national, world, and Olympic titles and is a huge star. Kulik probably does not have as high

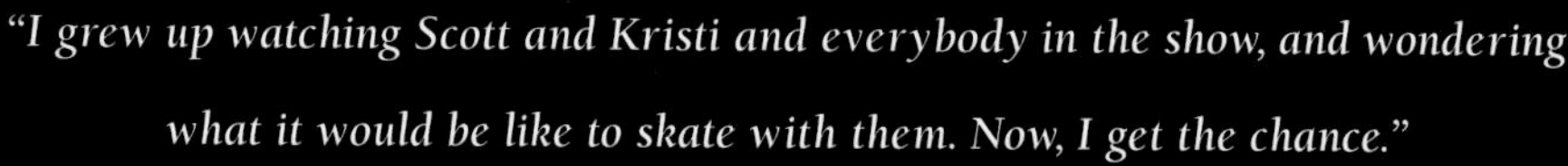

"I grew up watching Scott and Kristi and everybody in the show, and wondering what it would be like to skate with them. Now, I get the chance."

ILIA KULIK

a profile as a Todd Eldredge or maybe even an Elvis Stojko. But he is an incredible talent, and our feeling is his star will rise just like Kurt's has."

Those two impressive additions were joined by the elegant Lu Chen, winner of the bronze medal in the two most recent Olympics.

"Lu Chen was in many ways the story of the Olympics," Allen said. "She was the world champion in 1995, had a great performance in '96 to finish second, and then—because of injuries and other things—fell off sharply. And after all that, to come back to give the kind of performance she did at Nagano was so heart-warming and fantastic."

And along with the perky teenager came Russian Ilia Kulik, whose victory at the Nagano Games was highlighted by the most difficult free skate ever seen.

Also signed were three-time U.S. pair champions Jenni Meno and Todd Sand, fresh off a second-place showing at the world championships. Ironically, Meno and Sand's career actually slumped after they married each other, and they struggled with jumps in competition. But their smooth, classical style and unique lifts made them a prime commodity for any tour, and Stars on Ice was fortunate to land them.

Finally, England's Steven Cousins, who appeared on the Canadian Stars on Ice show in 1997, joined the full tour. The sharp sense of humor he shows in his skating has been compared to Kurt and Scott, and never being a medalist in major Olympic-eligible events has in no way diminished his entertainment skills.

"Lu Chen was in many ways the story of the Olympics," Allen said. "She was the world champion in 1995, had a great performance in '96 to finish second, and then—because of injuries and other things—fell off sharply. And after all that, to come back to give the kind of performance she did at Nagano was so heartwarming and fantastic."

LU CHEN

Also signed were three-time U.S. pair champions Jenni Meno and Todd Sand. . . . Their smooth, classical style and unique lifts made them a prime commodity for any tour, and Stars on Ice was fortunate to land them.

ILIA KULIK

JENNI MENO & TODD SAND

Tara, with her youthful innocence and exuberance, spoke of the thrill of skating "with my idols."

"I joined with Stars because it is a great opportunity waiting for me," she continued, "and it's time for me to expand artistically. And doing those group numbers will be so much fun. I've watched the show for years and that has been my favorite thing.

"I grew up watching Scott and Kristi and everybody in the show, and wondering what it would be like to skate with them. Now, I get the chance."

TARA LIPINSKI

. . .England's Steven Cousins, who appeared on the Canadian Stars on Ice show in 1997, joined the full tour. The sharp sense of humor he shows in his skating has been compared to Kurt and Scott. . . .

STEVEN COUSINS

PHOTO CREDITS

Allsport Photography—14, 15, 16, 24, 28, 29, 30, 34, 110, 111, 155, 156, 157, 158, 159

AP Worldwide Photos—150

David Baden Personal Photos—100, 103, 104, 105, 134

Dino Ricci—9, 38, 53, 56, 60, 65, 90, 91, 93

Ekaterina Gordeeva Personal Photos—27, 74, 114, 115, 117, 122, 123, 128,

Ernie Lebya—23, 29, 79

Heinz Kluetmeier—2, 6, 10, 32, 39, 40, 41, 43, 46, 47, 49, 51, 52, 54, 55, 57, 58, 59, 61, 62, 64, 65, 66, 67, 68, 69, 70, 71, 72, 73, 75, 76, 77, 78, 80, 81, 83, 84, 86, 87, 88, 89, 92, 94, 95, 96, 97, 98, 99, 102, 106, 107, 109, 115, 116, 118, 119, 121, 125, 127, 129, 135, 136, 137, 138, 139, 141, 144, 145, 146, 147, 148,149, 152

Hoffman Photography—151

IMG Archives—13, 31, 36, 42, 50, 79, 140, 153

Ingrid Butt —35, 112

Karen Kresge Personal Photos—19

Lea Ann Miller Personal Photos—21, 45

Lynn Plage Personal/Publicity Photos—17, 26, 37, 85, 101, 113

Neil Zlozower—33

Photo Design—25

Michael Sterling Publicity—131, 132

Sports Illustrated—133

Yuki Saegusa Personal Photos—18, 20, 38